S0-BKI-786

Ask Jackie

Animals

Copyright 1999-2012
ISBN: 978-0-9860152-0-5

Backwoods Home Magazine
PO Box 712
Gold Beach, Oregon 97444
www.backwoodshome.com

Edited by Jessie Denning, Julia Denning, Haley Kessel,
Connie Sayler, Lisa Nourse, Rhoda Denning, and Ilene Duffy
Cover art by Don Childers
Illustrations by Don Childers, Jessie Denning, and John Dean

Contents

Introduction

Nearly every homestead will have at least some critters, be they chickens, rabbits, or a dairy goat or two. The
amount of land a family has determines, to a great extent,
the variety and number of these animals. For instance, a
homesteading family on an acre of land can seldom spare
the room to house a dairy cow and her calf. But they sure
have room for a flock of chickens, a small rabbitry, and a
couple of milk goats.

These animals contribute greatly to the self-reliant
homestead. Chickens and other poultry provide eggs,
meat, and valuable manure for the garden. They are easy
to house and handle. Besides, they are fun to watch and
interact with!

Rabbits are quiet, gentle, and easily handled by even
the most timid homesteader and their children. They also
provide tasty meat and valuable manure.

Dairy goats require a little more forethought as they
have greater requirements such as: sturdy fencing, a
modest shelter, and a milking stand for ease of milking.
In exchange, they give you not only milk but also cheese,
cottage cheese, yogurt, and ice cream. An added bonus
is meat from castrated male kids or cash from the sale of
wether or doe kids. Your garden will also love goats, as
their manure is excellent organic fertilizer.

Nearly any homestead can raise a pig or two to butcher.
A butcher hog requires little space. A couple hundred
square feet, well managed, can corral a pig, and a simple
shelter is all a hog requires. In as little as six months'
time a weaned pig will weigh about 250-285 pounds and

be ready to butcher. This is about the fastest weight gain of any meat animal.

Of course, if you have a larger acreage you can easily raise a bottle calf to butchering size. But it will take the calf nearly two years' time — as well as adequate pasture, hay, and grain — to reach 1,000 pounds. In the end though, you'll have a great deal (about 700 pounds!) of the best-tasting beef imaginable.

Both the butcher pig and steer also will give you plenty of manure to add to your garden's compost pile. It's a totally win-win situation.

In this book, I answer a whole lot of common (and a few uncommon) questions folks have asked about a wide variety of homestead critters. Have fun reading and I hope I answer some of your own questions along the way.

— Jackie Clay

Chickens

Inbreeding chickens

How long can you keep the same rooster without your flock becoming inbred? Or are there any inbreeding problems with chickens?

Heather Adams, Oregon

It depends on whether or not you are saving chicks to use as adult layers. If you do, it's a good idea to trade roosters with a friend every three years or so. While inbreeding is not a huge issue with a home flock, too much inbreeding can result in some congenital problems. If you aren't letting hens go broody and hatch eggs, the same rooster can be kept for years and years.

In fact, a rooster is not necessary at all unless you *do* plan on having fertile eggs to hatch or use. A lot of urban chicken owners have a small flock of hens for home use, but don't keep a rooster so their neighbors won't complain of the early morning crowing.

Broody chicken

I have a chicken who is one broody girl. Just fine with me as we still have some time left this season for some new chicks.

My question is may I move her from the coop with all her eggs or should I move her over without her eggs and just put some in here and there on top of the new ones she lays? I have several that can go under her right now and would sure love her help. She doesn't let me get near the ones she is sitting on at night, so I was hoping to move her and her eggs over to a safe place out of the main coop. Would this work? Will she still sit on them?

Christine Wasankari, Washington

Yes, she'll still sit on them.

The easiest way to set a broody hen is to move her and her eggs (or the eggs you wish her to set on) into an enclosed box at night. Cover the box for a couple of days, then remove the cover; she should be set tight. Be sure to have food and water available to her. The best way I've found is to make a small "chicken tractor" with a nest box she can be locked in at first. After she's set tight, open the door and let her have free range to go out and eat and drink as she needs to. Then when the chicks hatch, they have a protected environment to grow in.

Cannibalistic chickens

We are having problems in the chicken coop with beak pecking — kind of cannibalistic. I think I remember hearing that you could trim chicken beaks to help prevent this. Do you know what this entails and how to safely do this? Or any other suggestions? The chickens haven't been out of the pen for several weeks now with the severe weather here in northern Minnesota this winter — maybe they are bored cooped up!

Debra Brown, Minnesota

You *can* trim the upper beak of chickens to reduce cannibalism, but this is quite severe. It is done with a cauterizing cutter, as you trim back to where there is blood supply; without the cauterization, it would bleed. I would remove any chickens with any bloody pecked areas. Then let the chickens outside, even for a few hours in the afternoon. It's amazing what this will do for them; they peck snow, flap around, and enjoy themselves, totally forgetting boredom and pecking. Giving them something special to peck on also helps: a squash, cabbage, head of lettuce, trimmings from the store (free). Soon the weather will turn nice again and they can be out all day, as they wish. And the pecking usually stops. Reintroduce the pecked chickens after they have healed, putting them in at night so the others don't notice the newbie.

Chickens picking at each other

I know chickens are omnivores, but why do they pick at each other — is something lacking in their diet?

Donald Allen, Texas

Chickens develop this habit, usually, from boredom. Be sure they can get outside daily, even in bad weather. Also give them plenty of room both inside and out. Giving them such things as soaked alfalfa leaves or rabbit pellets, fresh greens, and also scattering some grain outside so they can dig and scratch will also help prevent this problem. Remove any chicken that has a spot picked so bad that it is bleeding; chickens will pick such a bird so badly that it will eventually die. Once the bird is healed, it is okay to put it back into the coop.

Rooster acting strange

I have a hen and a rooster (supposed to be two hens — HAH!) and when I approach the rooster he has taken to squatting down with his head down until I pet him, as if he is showing me obeisance! This is disturbing to me and I wonder if I can release him from the need. The hen doesn't do it. Can you explain this to me? They are Buff Orpingtons and even the rooster is sweet.

Alice Hood, Arizona

He just sees you as the dominant "rooster." I'm thinking that when he gets older, he'll probably re-think that and become a "normal" rooster. It's nothing to worry about; he should outgrow it.

How long will hens be productive?

How long can I keep chickens in order that they be productive for eggs? How many years are they good for laying eggs? Does it depend on the type of chickens? Some are better layers than others. Mine are mainly Ameraucanas.

Peter Yaruchyk, Indiana

Commercial chickens are only kept for one year. But most homesteaders keep their laying hens for longer. I have some that are six years old and still laying decently. Ameraucanas are often long-lived layers, where some of the commercial breeds, such as leghorns, seem to lay themselves into an early chicken soup.

Coccidiosis

What are the symptoms of a hen with an egg stuck in her vent? What can be done to "unstick" it? I have lost six hens in the past two years, all of them less than two years old. There are signs of diarrhea that I treated with antibiotics, to no avail. I am stumped as to what it could be.

Ellen Kelling Vukovic, Wisconsin

If a hen is egg bound she will sit in her nest box and strain for a long period; she may also have a red or prolapsed vent. When you suspect an egg bound hen, you can usually correct the problem by injecting about 10 ccs of warmed oil, such as olive or mineral oil, up into the vent using a syringe. The stuck egg will usually come out quite quickly.

Diarrhea isn't usually a symptom of a hen being egg bound. Chickens are quite prone to coccidiosis, which does cause diarrhea. I'd suggest taking a fresh sample of one of the hen's manure to your vet and having it checked for coccidiosis. It is usually easily treated by putting medication in the drinking water. Be sure to keep a clean run and coop; a yucky run encourages coccidiosis.

Poultry parasites

My question is about all your poultry. Do you worry about parasites in the poultry such as round worms? Do you worm them at all? If so, what do you use and how often? I know you have a variety of ages and your turkeys are in with the chickens in the winter. Plus you have other animals that could have parasites in the poop which the chickens could pick at.

Cindy Hills, Wisconsin

Despite all the poop the chickens pick at, it's amazing to discover that chickens and other poultry are really quite resistant to having worms as opposed to other farm animals, such as horses and goats. No, we don't worm our poultry. Every few years we have a few fecal samples checked, but so far we have had no parasites. (The only way to know for sure if your birds or animals have internal parasites is to have your veterinarian check fecal samples under a microscope.)

Molting chickens

We have 8 layers, 2 each of Barred Rock, Rhode Island Red, New Hampshire Red, and Araucana. They are 1½ years old.

After molting, only one of them has regrown tail-feathers completely and all of them have featherless areas on their nether parts. The skin looks like the red rubber ball we all played with in grade school. I have examined them closely and see no evidence of small mites or other crawlies. I do see them peck at each others' feathers, but is this normal?

They really don't look that appealing. We have 13 new babies (7 weeks old) in a separate area of the coop, but I hesitate to mix them for fear of this featherless situation.

Kirsten Hollenbeck, Oregon

I think your hens are just not finished molting. My own flock looks pretty scruffy right now, too. I have partially bald hens, hens with blue quills sticking every which way where the new feathers are coming in, and hens with pimply butts as red as your chickens'. But I know in a few weeks they'll all look beautiful again. Yours will too.

Hen lost her feathers

I have four 3-4 year old hens. One has lost her feathers around her neck and chest. This has been ongoing without change for approximately six months. The other hens are not affected. She is otherwise healthy and happy. Recently, her green eggs have developed dark colored spots on them. There is no rooster in the group. Initially I thought she was battling to replace a rooster's position. I have not seen any indication of this. I am in a hot, desert climate. I want to bring more young hens home but want to know what's wrong with her first.

Pamalyn Peterson, Nevada

Your hen may have feather mites. If you look very closely on the "bald" spots, you may see tiny moving insects on the skin or feather shafts. Although ugly, this is seldom serious.

Get some rotenone powder from your garden center or feed mill (make sure it is labeled for animal use, too), then hold her upside down by her legs. Dust her well, then do your other hens, as they may be infested but not show feather loss. The feathers should start growing back within a month's time. As for the dark spots on the eggs, I wouldn't worry about that at all.

Escaping hen for dinner

I have 15 White Rock chickens, first ones I've had since I was a kid. Two roosters, 13 hens. I have one hen who is insistent on getting out of my fenced lot (1.5 acres).

I'm trying to decide; I have, I think, two choices ... 1. put her in the crock pot before the rest of the flock decides she's got a good idea 2. let the neighbor's large Labrador have her (this dog is VERY interested in any chicken that is close to the fence); or, a coyote or fox.

Inside the fence I have three dogs; outside, she has no protection, so I'm thinkin' it's just a matter of time. I've already scooped her up with a fishing net once this morning; she went right back over before I had the net hung up in the garage. I gave the rest of the flock some feed and put them in the pen while I'm trying to figure out if I should just let nature take its course.

Also, thanks to you for getting me into canning; I had not thought to put in a raised bed, but your discussions got me started.

Elton Wylie, Texas

I would probably plan on chicken and dumplings for dinner next week.

The only other option would be to secure your fence. No chicken, no matter how determined, can force through a well built fence. And White Rocks can't fly worth a darned, either.

I've had crappy fences in the past and they were a pain in the neck; someone was always getting out and into places I didn't want them. Let me tell you, a good fence is a thing of joy!

Setting eggs

My grandmother, "Ma Bessie," always set her hens with the moon but I can't remember anything else about setting hens other than she would keep about 12 eggs and put them under one hen. How do you know which hen? How do you know where the moon is? I really want to raise my own chicks but have no clue how to. Can you give me step by step instructions on this process? Also can I leave the chicks in with the flock after they hatch or do I need to separate them from the flock? I think "Ma" left them in.

Nancy Burton, Ohio

As to how many eggs to set under a hen, it kind of depends on the hen. Large hens, such as cochins, can handle a dozen eggs. Smaller and younger hens, less than that. You want to have the hen able to totally cover all the eggs at one time. My little bantam hen can only handle seven full-sized eggs. I've never set my eggs by the moon, although I know people who swear by it. I set my eggs under a broody hen when I want some chicks. A broody hen is usually an older hen who has been laying and then decides she wants to set. She will take over a nest box, refusing to get off eggs that are under her ... even if it is only an egg or two from today's laying. She'll fluff up her feathers and "growl" at you ... even peck when you reach under her or try to move her out of the nest. Often she'll stay in the box even if you take the eggs out from under her. When I have a broody hen, I usually put my chosen eggs under her in the evening and place a wire front or even a slat in front of the nest so the other hens don't try to lay eggs in that nest. Hens crowding into the nest with her will not only lay more eggs in the nest, but they may break the setting eggs. I usually keep the hen and her brood separate for a few days so the older hens don't pick on the babies. I also do this as the very young chicks will drown in the big chickens' waterer. Of course you can put marbles or stones in the waterer so they won't drown and watch for picking. I have raised batches of chicks right in with the flock with no problems. You'll just have to watch and see how yours do. Good luck! It's really fun to see the little fuzzy guys following the momma around the yard, learning to peck, run, and fly.

What breed of chicken?

I bought a straight run of chickens from my local Tractor Supply about a month ago. I am trying to determine the breed because no one at the store seemed to know for sure. I estimate their age at 8 weeks. They are white in color and seem large for their age. I believe they are Cornish Rocks or possibly Cornish Cross (due to their size). How can I know for sure?

Stephen Maynard, West Virginia

You probably have Cornish Rocks or "meat chickens." They are the most commonly found chicks on the market today because they grow so quickly. This is your clue. They have thick yellow legs and really get huge fast. Don't do like I did, though, and keep a few as breeders. Every single one I have done this with had the legs/feet go bad;

they just can't stand the weight. Butcher them and you'll have the best and most meat possible!

Chickens in the city

I live on the outer edge of the city; backyard is fenced in by 6-foot high privacy fence, neighbors on two sides, none in back or ever will be. I have a space in rear corner of yard about 12x12 feet that I would like to put chickens in. We use approximately 2 dozen eggs a week.

Which chickens are the quietest, best layers, and how many do I need? I was thinking 4. No rooster allowed, too noisy.

I really don't want to use laying mash because of hormones and other additives. Will the hens lay sufficiently without it?

Richard L. Anderson, Georgia

Any of the heavy breeds are quite docile and calm, especially cochins (but they aren't as good an egg layer as, say, Buff Orphingtons or Rhode Island Reds). Hens are pretty quiet, as a rule, singing and clucking as they go about their business. The only time there's noise is when they lay an egg or something is chasing them — then they'll loudly cackle and squawk. Most heavy hens will lay an egg a day during the spring and summer, then taper off to maybe an egg every other day during the fall and winter (if you keep a light on for them for a few extra hours during the short-day period). But realistically, there are just days they don't lay, especially during the two molting periods they go through every year. So you have to take this into consideration.

You don't need a rooster unless you want to hatch eggs and need fertile ones.

Yes, hens will lay without laying mash. I don't feed it to my hens and they do fine. But I do give them plenty of greens year-round, as well as house scraps and goat milk when I have it. Hens will lay more on laying mash, but will have a longer useful life without it.

Be sure your neighbors will not be against your new project. Perhaps a promise of fresh eggs every once in a while (your extras) would make them more agreeable to having chicken neighbors. It often works that way.

Moving to the farm

We are preparing to retire from the city to my family farm — in the family since about 1880. Money will be tight with all of us going back to the land, so this needs to be economical and not cost us more to produce than to buy at the store. There is a nice house and one huge hay barn a good distance from the house, but no buildings remain for small animals. My mother has been living there and wanted nothing to do with small livestock.

We want to have chickens and possibly dairy goats. But the economics of keeping both seem high to our preliminary checking. I have never had chickens but my grandmothers of course had them up until I was in my 20s. I personally have raised Spanish and Cashmere goats but never dairy. We live in Texas. We will have 240 acres — but it has been converted to primarily coastal pasture for a cow/calf operation (dad was a beef cattle expert) — which we are not sure is the direction we want to go. We will be starting from scratch on chicken and goat housing.

My questions are for the most economical ways to:

1. Feed chickens — layer formulas seem very expensive.

2. Buy litter for the chicken house for easy cleaning — also seems expensive. Hay is expensive — straw not really available in this part of the country as I see up north.

3. Keep chickens safe — predators will be a huge problem, especially neighbors' large dogs allowed to run freely.

We will have a good gardening area (the only downside is it is like beach sand and will need extensive composting) and I believe there are a number of things we can grow to help feed the chickens and goats. I am considering the two-sided chicken setup where you run chickens on one side one year and garden on the other. Then reverse. We appreciate any tips you have. I know this can be done.

Susan Ginnings, Texas

Yes, you're right. This *can* be done. You just have to think outside the box. First of all, yes, layer mash is expensive. But you can also feed your chickens plain old scratch feed, supplemented with weeds, kitchen waste, garden waste, extra vegetables, and even pasture, if your chicken yard is big enough. We let our chickens free range and they only get a little scoop of feed twice a day, to keep them near the buildings. They forage, eating grasshoppers, ticks, caterpillars, and all sorts of greens, seeds, and other natural foods they run across. I also give them any extra goat milk, whey, etc., from my goats, as it boosts their protein very inexpensively.

I like your idea of switching gardening and chicken yards; it works great, providing your gardening areas are big enough to make a productive self-sustaining garden. We are going to let our hens run on our new orchard, which is also planted to clover. This orchard is 100x175 feet, roughly. The chicken manure will help fertilize it; the clover, grasses, and insects will help feed the hens. *And* the 6-foot high 2x4 fence will keep out any wandering predators. This is a much better fence than chicken wire. But if you have stray dogs, you might want to reinforce that fence with a couple of strands of electric wire. They will *not* jump against the fence more than once!

As for litter, maybe you could find a carpenter or lumberyard that would give you leftover sawdust. This makes good bedding, and is usually free for the hauling. Ground corncobs, leaves, and even dried lawn clippings also make great bedding. Right now, I'm buying bales of pine shavings until we get more established, but I only buy a bale every 2-3 weeks and I have 24 hens, two roosters, and two turkeys in the same coop. Of course, I'll be eliminating that expense very soon!

Hens eating eggs

I have a medium-sized flock of 25 chickens. They started to lay only after 4-4½ months old! My problem now is they have taken a liking to eating the eggs. We were getting around 15 eggs a day, but now we sometimes only get 6 because they ate the rest! The coop is very large, and they have a very large run. We also have more nesting boxes than most say they need, so I don't think they are crowded.

Recently we tried giving them some meat protein (scraps from the two mule deer we harvested this season) and it seemed to slow down the egg eating, only about 1-3 a day. Their diet consists of layer pellets, scrap veggies from a local restaurant (raw lettuce and tomatoes), and leftover breads from the local Christian mission, plus weeds and such from the garden. I've also tried the golf ball solution, but no cigar.

Dave Rose, Colorado

Unfortunately, chickens *do* like to eat eggs. But to keep more for yourself, collect the eggs as often as you can — up to several times daily until the problem abates. You can also try using ceramic or wooden nest eggs, which work better than golf balls. If they still do it, consider using a new nest box that has roll-outs, so that when a hen lays her egg and gets up, the egg rolls gently out of the nest box to a secure location. Other than these tips, a one-way trip to the chopping block will cure the problem permanently, but it's an expensive "cure" for all involved!

Integrating chickens

We lost 5 chickens several weeks ago to our dog. We have one Black Australorp hen (a little over 7 months old) whose roommate was killed. We have tried to re-integrate her with the original flock and they try to kill her every time. If we get another hen to keep her company, should we quarantine that hen for a while before putting it with our hen? The sale barn we would go to tests all the poultry ahead of time, before they are sold. None of our birds are vaccinated, all their housing is new, and there have never been other birds on our place.

Julia Rader, Arkansas

It's always safest to quarantine a chicken that's been in unknown conditions or even if they have just come back from a fair or poultry show. It is rare to have a new bird come into your flock bringing disease, but it can happen.

Ask Jackie

Feeding milk to chickens

I've recently read about the possibility of "souring milk" to create chicken feed. Can't really find any instructions on doing that and am wondering if you've ever heard of or know of a recipe to do that?

James Gilliland, Texas

Sour milk, fed to chickens, is usually just house milk that has gone sour by itself. You can also feed them regular, unsoured milk. I do it all the time, and the chickens sure like it, plus it helps on the feed bill, too. But if you want to sour it first, just set it out at room temperature until it clabbers, or pour in half a cup of vinegar for quick clabbering.

Feeding poultry milk

Jackie, did you say that your poultry likes fresh goat milk? And you feed it to them regularly? I don't have a dairy goat but was considering the uses of goat milk. Plus, I just like critters. I have been studying on Nigerian Dwarf dairy goats. Would one goat be content among other poultry? And no other goats?

Joanna Wilcox, North Carolina

Yes! My poultry (ducks, turkeys, and chickens) love goat milk, along with the whey from cheese and buttermilk from butter making. While goats are herd animals, they will learn to bond with you and also any other critters you have and will be quite content, as long as you pay some attention to them on a regular basis. You probably won't want to house her right in their coop/pen. Goats tend to get pooped on as poultry think of goats as nice roosts, complete with foot warmers.

Goat milk too good to waste on chickens

Joanna Wilcox (Ask Jackie, Issue 115, Jan/Feb 2009) does not appear to understand in her letter that goats are not poultry. I am 84 years old. Growing up I was told goat milk was for drinking. It tastes the best as it comes from the goat nice and warm. The chickens that learned to nurse got some milk but the majority drank water. It's too good to waste on the chickens.

M.D. Ecker, Connecticut

I've got to catch those chickens that are smart enough to nurse! So there's where that milk is going! Seriously, though, I do feed some extra milk to my chickens, and whey from cheese making. It saves on expensive feed and provides them with tons of nutrition.

Garden scraps for chickens

We have recently moved to our homestead, started a garden, and acquired chickens. My question is: after we harvest our potatoes (which are doing really well!), can we safely feed the potato plants (stems and leaves) to the chickens? I have found conflicting information on this topic, I hope you can help. If it is not safe to feed the potato plants to the chickens, what do you do with them? Can you safely put the plants in the compost bin? Are there any other vegetable plants that might be a problem to feed to the chickens?

Brenda Palmer, Washington

There is a neat website on this subject, www.Poultry-Help.com. It's best not to feed tomato or potato plants as they do contain toxins that may harm chickens or animals (although the deer sure ate ours!). We simply till our spent potato and tomato plants into the garden soil, unless they show signs of disease, such as spotted, yellow leaves. In this case, we burn our dry plants in an isolated spot away from our garden to avoid spreading disease into our soil and future plants.

Grain mix for laying hens

Could you give us a recipe or ratio for grains to feed our egg-laying chickens? A ratio would be great. Be sure to include grit, oyster shell, vitamins, minerals, etc. if they would benefit the birds. As you can probably tell, we are complete novices at raising chickens but we are having loads of fun trying. Wish we had started sooner. These guys are really entertaining. We bought some Barred Rocks, supposed to be pullets but ended up with one cockerel in the bunch and we are delighted. He is not fully grown yet but likes to supervise "his girls." My grandson named him Abraham (the father of many nations).

We bought the book on chickens and really appreciate all the valuable info in it. We have since branched out and ordered some Cornish Cross chicks for meat and they are really growing. I can see why they are ready to butcher in six weeks.

Joyce Baum, Missouri

Chickens are *very* easy to feed so they can lay lots of eggs, make lots of meat, and stay healthy. I've never used a recipe or grain mix I carefully managed. I start with a good quality 18% ground oats/corn/wheat poultry feed from our mill, then add all the bugs and vegetable matter (clover, grass, weeds, seeds, etc.) they can eat from in our orchard, plus kitchen and garden scraps and whatever goat milk we might have left. They thrive on it! If you want tons of scientific information on feeding chickens, go online to www.ThePoultrySite.com.

Do be careful with your Cornish Cross chicks as they grow larger. I do not feed commercial meat grower formula as it puts on *too* much size and fat; the chickens' legs go out on them and they are prone to heart attacks — both fatal conditions. Either butcher them at 6-8 weeks, or if you hold them longer, be sure to ease off the meat grower and corn to prevent these conditions.

Worms as chicken feed

I use redworms to compost waste products; everything from plant materials to animal and human manures. In my part of Interior Alaska, earthworms are not native and they don't survive our weather extremes without special care. Those I can't provide for die off quickly. So there is little benefit to be had from turning them out with the compost.

Still, I have begun to wonder if turning them out this way is utilizing my worms to their fullest value. Do you remember the "worm cookie" craze of the early 70s? Worm "flour" was touted as being very high in protein. Currently I have to supplement my home grown chicken feed with protein pellets during the winter or no eggs. It doesn't take much so it's not a huge expense, but it's money out of pocket just the same. I am considering the possibility of using the worms in place of the pellets.

Obviously, it would not be a good idea to use them raw. I don't want to infect my stock with parasites or pathogens.

But I wouldn't want to overcook the worms and diminish their food value either. Also I would like to store them for winter use.

So, my questions are:

1. Do you know how to process these worms into a safe, palatable feed for my chickens?

2. What would be the food value of worms so processed? Would they be a valuable enough source of protein to be worth my while?

Hope you're not laughing too hard to help me.

Susan Nilsson, Alaska

Okay, good questions. First of all, you could simply bake these worms for half an hour at 350°F in your oven. But the house will stink like you would not believe. Been there, done that. Not on purpose, but while sterilizing garden soil for seed starting. This will render them wholesome and safe.

Food value? About the same as any meat by-product. However, I really don't think it would be worthwhile, time wise, to pursue this avenue. In the same time it would take you to cook, dry, and store these worms, you could probably earn enough to buy your protein pellets.

Have you considered giving your chickens milk during the winter? This improves the protein content of the feed and stimulates them to eat more, thus more eggs. The additional calcium in the milk also helps build good shells. If you have a milk goat or access to extra milk, you might give that a try.

You can keep worms over winter by keeping them in a bin. Dig down 18 inches into the soil, removing the soil from an area four feet by four feet. Lay a two-inch thick piece of foam insulation down and add your nice compost and soil mixed. Then add your worms and a good layer of leaves. On top of this, stack two layers of hay or straw bales. I've done this and pulled away a bale of straw on a sunny way-sub-zero day only to find nice fat worms crawling just below the bale.

Chicken feed

Thanks for the scratch-feed idea in issue 88. I didn't know that was an option, and have been feeding chick starter for new chicks, grower for the older chicks, and mash for the laying hens. I have found a mash without meat by-products in it, although it has fish meal. Is that any better than what you have seen produced? I've become frustrated this season trying to keep separate all the different ages of birds and their respective feeds, seeing as the older birds would rather steal in and eat the baby food. I've wondered what farmers 100 years ago fed their chicks. What do you feed yours? Do you grind up the scratch feed so that it's easier for the babies, or do you feed starter and the like? I'm ready to switch to one feed for all ages, but don't want to short-change anybody. As we live in north-central Minnesota, would you recommend adding anything to the scratch (other than vegetable scraps) for the chickens in the winter?

Faye Lilyerd

I start my hatchery baby chicks on commercial chick starter, but as soon as they feather out and become more active, I switch them to scratch feed. To boost up the protein, they also get lots of goat milk and whey from cheese making. They have a pan of it in front of them, just as they do water. It does attract flies in the summer, but the chicks snap them up for dessert.

In the old days, farmers would start their chicks on coarsely ground grains soaked in milk, buttermilk, and whey, along with mashed hard boiled eggs. This works fine. I've done it but it is labor intensive.

My northern Minnesota chickens got scratch feed for 20 years, summer and winter. And they still do. But I do supplement it with vegetable scraps, soaked alfalfa pellets (or fine hay leaves), and milk. They come through the winter in fine shape. If you are pushing for egg production, as do commercial flocks, this will not produce a copious number of eggs. But it will supply a homestead nicely.

Corn cobs for chicken feed

We grow a lot of corn in our garden. We also have a few chickens. I was wondering if there was any nutritional value in grinding corn cobs for chicken feed?

Marsha Pagenkopf, Kansas

No, not really. I let my chickens pick all the corn they can salvage from the green cobs after I've cut off corn to can or dehydrate. They do get a lot of food this way … as well as entertainment. You should see my hens run when it's canning time and I head for the run with a pail of corn cobs!

Ground cobs for chickens

On reading Ask Jackie in Issue #132, I began an urgent letter to you, but it only got as far as "Dear Jackie" when a dire family crisis hit the fan, and it was two months later that I finally got back to the typewriter. I hope the delay didn't cost any innocent chicken lives!

Marsha Pagenkopf, of Kansas, inquired about ground corn cobs as chicken feed. You apparently took her to mean fresh green cobs, which of course are harmless and supply a little food value. (But did you ever try to grind any?) I took Marsha to mean dry cob meal, which is added to cattle feed as a filler and has some nutritive value to a cow. However, cob meal is sure death to chickens! They can't digest it, not even when soaked in water; in fact, wetting it speeds the death of the birds, which starve with grossly distended crops.

I lost an entire flock of lovely pullets when my son, thinking old Mom didn't know what she was talking about, ignored my careful instructions to put only shelled corn in the feed mix, threw in "just a few sacks" of whole ear corn to save me a few cents.

When I filled the feeders with the new batch, my pullets at first refused to eat it. (Smarter than my son!) It was much too fine ground, and I thought this must be why they didn't like it; not having any money for more feed, I said "Sorry, girls, this is all there is, get used to it" and they did eat it, very reluctantly leaving most of it. I tried making a thin slop of it with water, which they devoured frantically, but this only hastened their death. Only after all 50 birds were dead or near it, did my son confess what he had done. He paid for a new batch of chicks, and fed the feed to his cattle, but that did little to balance the loss to me.

I hope someone tipped off Marsha before she suffered the same loss; and that you will tell your readers the full story.

Phyl Hubbard, Indiana

Ask Jackie

(Editor's note: We called Marsha as soon as we got your letter.)

Thanks for sharing your experience! There is a regional difference as to what is meant by cob meal. Out west, cob is an abbreviation for corn, oats, and barley, and it is often fed to chickens. Here, in the north, there *is* no cob meal, period. So please, readers, don't feed your chickens ground corn cobs, thinking to save a buck.

Seeds for chicken feed

I have a variety of banana that is cold-hardy but inedible because of its numerous seeds the size of popcorn kernels in the fruit. Can you tell me if they would make good chicken feed if ground in my grain mill?

Do you know of any other seeds of fruits that I may be throwing away that would be useful chicken feed?

Joe Pool, Louisiana

You can certainly feed your banana seeds to your chickens. They would eat the whole fruit, except the peel, as well. The seeds do not need to be ground. Just about any fruit seeds; orange, lemon, grapefruit, apple, grape, pear, and others are relished by chickens. I keep a chicken pan on the counter. This is filled daily with "chicken scraps," which is a different container from the "dog scraps" that go to our Huskies. Chicken scraps contain crushed egg shells, potato peels, fruit peels and seeds, "old" bits of gelatin salad, salad greens, cabbage hearts, etc. The dog scraps include meat scraps (no bones), leftover pancakes, muffins, bread, soups, carrot peels, dribbles of cooking fat, etc. I may give either group leftover casseroles, mac and cheese, potato salad, stew, or whatever I clean out of my fridge that is not moldy.

Feed for chickens

A while back you mentioned that if we knew how they made laying mash, we wouldn't buy it. Is it bad for the chickens? Quite frankly, I don't have much leftovers to feed them (my husband is a big eater and loves my cooking.) In place of the mash, what should I buy instead? I plan on developing a small laying flock.

Kathy Lupole, New York

I don't feed my chickens laying mash. I don't like feeding dehydrated slaughterhouse waste products (interpret for yourself here) to birds who provide my eggs and sometimes meat. Yuck! Instead, I give them all my peelings, parings, over-the-edge fruit and vegetables, extra goat milk and whey, and any table scraps we have left. I also raise extra produce for them such as squash, carrots, apples, turnips, Swiss chard, etc. In the winter, I shake a leaf of alfalfa or clover hay onto a tarp, then pour boiling water over the leaves. This makes a nice warm chicken salad.

Winter chicken feed

I loved your article on chickens, but I have a question. In the winter, I've been told that I have to feed them a "winter mash." I've tried looking it up online and found the ingredients but it's things I can't get. What do you do? Do you have to feed them a special processed feed or can I make one at home myself?

Sera Waters, Florida

In the winter I feed the same feed as in the summer, but I also soak some alfalfa leaves or pellets in hot water overnight until it absorbs all the water, then dish it out to the girls. I also give them squash seeds and strings, potato peels, apple peels, carrot pieces, and other root cellar and kitchen scraps. They do just fine on this "winter mash."

Unmedicated feed

I am raising my first flock of chickens (White Rocks). When I went to my feed store I tried to find a commercial feed that wasn't medicated (antibiotics, etc.). I can't find any place in my area that sells unmedicated feed. What are my other options for noncommercial/unmedicated commercial feed?

Ryan Olsen, Idaho

You can use unmedicated duckling starter for starting chicks. This is usually available, although you may have to preorder before your chicks arrive. For older chicks and adults, why not just feed scratch feed? This is unmedicated, and is what we use. Antibiotics have their place, but I really believe that good husbandry practices far outshine stuffing antibiotics into poultry and animals as a substitute.

Broken egg shells

We have 6 red sex-link chickens. They're free range with a nice coop, we keep it clean. It's timer lit from 8 a.m. to 8 p.m. We feed them laying mash, cracked corn, ground shell, and bread once in a while for a treat. We've come to love them (go figure). They're in their second laying year.

Lately we've been finding broken eggs under their night perches. The shells are paper thin and pinkish. I can't find any info on it. We have your "Chickens: A Beginner's Handbook" and another, but there's no mention. Can you tell us what's causing this?

Donna Summerville, West Virginia

Stress sometimes causes this, but the usual cause is lack of calcium and vitamin D3. I'd give them oyster shell (free choice), and add poultry vitamins to the drinking water. Giving them some greens sometimes helps this too. I feed our flock leftover lettuce and cabbage greens as well as giving them alfalfa chaff, soaked overnight in boiling water, several times a week when they can't get out onto green pasture. This is a common occurrence and can usually be remedied within a couple of weeks' time.

Homemade chicken feed

How can I make my own chicken feed? I have three laying hens and I have no idea what is in that junk I buy at the feed store. I would like to make my own, in 50-100 lb. batches and then scoop it out and put it through the food processor as needed. The easier the recipe and fewer the ingredients, the better.

Erica Leake

Well, you could make your own chicken feed, but what I do is buy scratch feed, which is simply cracked corn, wheat, and milo. I do not buy laying mash, because I've seen it made. You don't want to know what's in it. Scratch feed is not supposed to be a "complete" feed, but my chickens are on free range all day long, and they also eat up household scraps and gardening surplus. I've never seen any sort of nutritional deficiency in my poultry, and they lay very well, indeed. You do not have to grind the feed. Chickens with adequate grit (either commercial or simply picked up in the yard) can handle whole grains. The cracked corn simply is easier for them to peck. It's a good idea to supply your hens with oyster shell, as well to help them build nice thick egg shells.

If your hens are confined, give them daily snacks such as weeds and excess garden or table scraps and they'll do fine.

Keeping eggs fresh

My family and I are getting ready to buy our first chickens. I am worried about storing the eggs. We don't have a huge fridge and I am worried about bacteria. My husband says you can keep eggs out for periods of time, but I am still worried. It must be my nurse's brain …

Cathy Rogers, Oklahoma

As long as the eggs are not cracked, fresh eggs will keep at cool room temperature for at least two weeks. After all, hens lay an egg a day, and lay about a dozen or more eggs before setting on them. If they'll develop a chick, they certainly won't be "bad" and make you sick. Remember, eggs won't develop an embryo unless they are fertile and held at 99.5 degrees. If your household "cool" temperature is that warm, you'd better refrigerate your eggs.

Can I freeze the eggs?

I am the happy owner of 20 beautiful hens and 2 dashing roosters. My question is this, is there a way to long-term store the eggs? Can I freeze them any way? Also, what is the breeding and gestation time for hens? My roosters are breeding now and I would rather the hens not go broody until warmer weather. Could you help shed some light?

Sherry Preedy, Kansas

Yes, you can freeze eggs. Most folks just break the eggs, several at a time, into small plastic freezer boxes. You want enough eggs to just about fill the box, leaving room for expansion during freezing but not enough space to let a lot of air contact the eggs. You can leave them whole or mix the whites and yolks.

You don't have to worry about your hens. Roosters breed year-round, but hens very seldom go broody until summer hits. Their bodies know when it's time to sit on eggs, even when you provide them with artificial light in the winter.

Unrefrigerated eggs

How long can fresh eggs go without refrigeration? If I leave my hens in their safe pen area while we go on a weekend trip, are the eggs still safe to eat when we return? This unusually hot summer never became cooler than the low 80s at night, while the daytime was well over 100 degrees. How long are they safe at this temperature? How about if a brood hen adopts them — how long are they safe for eating?

Brenda McGuire, Texas

If eggs are not set on by a hen, they will remain good for about a week in relatively warm temperatures, although very high temps can sometimes cause them to go bad sooner. (When in doubt, just break them into a cup before using them. A good egg has a firm, nice yolk. A bad one has a runny yolk.) After all, hens lay a clutch of eggs before they sit on them to hatch them and the eggs hatch into chicks! They are plenty good to eat. Now if a hen starts to set those eggs, they begin developing into chicks and you wouldn't want to eat them. They wouldn't poison you, but you might not like eating embryos!

Storing eggs

What are the best/easiest ways to save chicken eggs? I'm getting 7 eggs a day now and I don't know what to do with them all.

Donnie McIlwain, New York

The best way to save extra eggs is to freeze them. Break several eggs into a freezer container (you can separate whites in one and yolks in another, if you wish), or put two eggs in a small bag and place several bags in one container (so when you want only two eggs, you don't have to thaw the whole works), then freeze.

Storing fresh eggs

How can I store fresh eggs when egg production is down and have fresh eggs during the holiday baking time?

Lois Hutson, Texas

You can encourage your hens to lay longer in the season by keeping extra light in the coop. Sometimes this only requires adding a west-facing window. Other methods include keeping a light in the coop. I know people living off-grid who buy solar walk lights and place them in the south and west windows of the chicken coop to charge, then they come on at dark, keeping the hens active and laying all evening. If you have electricity, keep a 40-watt lightbulb burning in the coop using a cheap timer for four hours after sundown, and you'll find your hens lay more eggs and lay them longer in the year. Also, keeping your coop wind-proof and warm will encourage laying.

When your "girls" begin to slow down, gather all the fresh clean eggs to store. Eggs are protected, naturally, by a thin external membrane. Therefore, when you wash or scrub the eggs, the membrane is washed off and the eggs will store for shorter periods of time. Store only naturally clean eggs. By storing them in a cardboard egg carton in the refrigerator, you can keep them quite a long time.

When we lived way remote and snowmobiled in and out seven months out of the year, we gathered up eggs in November which was as late as the girls produced. Storing them as above, the eggs generally lasted nearly until spring production kicked in. Of course, the older eggs should be broken first into a cup, because once in a while you'll get a bad one. You can tell these by the runny yolk, watery white, and ugly look.

You can keep eggs in waterglass, which is a solution of sodium silicate and water. The sodium silicate clogs up the pores of the egg and helps keep them for longer periods of time. Likewise, rubbing fresh, clean eggs with lard or shortening will help keep them longer. Keeping eggs is not much of a problem using the above methods, so I do not bother with waterglass. It is messy and there is hardly a nastier feeling than reaching into a crock of waterglass solution for an egg or two.

Powdered eggs

I'd like to know how to powder and store my own eggs.
Pat Fessler, Maryland

I'm sorry, but I don't feel that eggs are a food we should dehydrate, due to possible bacterial action. Eggs are the perfect incubator for bacteria such as salmonella, and under home conditions, I wonder if we could get the eggs dehydrated before they "went bad." I buy dehydrated egg powder.

Dried eggs

I have chickens and a lot of eggs. Is there any way to dry eggs at home? I have used dried eggs at the store, but would like to be able to make my own.

Kathy Bower, Kansas

We also have chickens, but I don't believe there is a safe way to home-dry eggs due to the possibility of salmonella or other bacterial contamination. This goes for milk as well. My hens generally lay all winter, but when they seem to be slacking off I gather several dozen clean, fresh eggs, pack them unwashed in cartons, and place them in a very cool area — refrigerator or back corner of a 40 degree winter pantry. These will nearly always last till the "girls" are laying abundantly in the spring. My dried eggs are on the shelf, just in case.

Washing fresh eggs

I have 17 hens and 3 roosters, all free roam. Do I wash fresh chicken eggs? I have heard there is a natural protection on the shells that can be washed off and make the eggs' shelf life shorter. Also, any other good tips for producing, handling and keeping my eggs would be appreciated.

Konnie, Washington

I only wash my fresh eggs when they have chicken poop or other unsavory things tracked upon them by untidy hens. It's true that eggs have a protective coating on them and washing removes it.

Give your girls plenty of fresh water, year-round, and plenty of clean kitchen scraps in the winter in addition to their regular winter diet. Add a small light to be kept on in their coop at all times or at least for several hours at night in the winter (this increases egg production during the dark months). Let them outside during the winter when they wish, and keep the coop warm and dry. They'll reward your efforts with plenty of eggs and happy chicken singing.

Washing eggs

Should I wash my farm eggs before I put them in the fridge? Do you put your eggs in the fridge?

Pam, Montana

I wash my eggs only if they're in need. Clean ones go right into the carton and into the fridge. I try not to use detergent unless they won't come clean as it removes the protective coating naturally on eggs. But I want my eggs clean, too. So if they are soiled, I use a nylon scrubby pad and a bit of dish detergent if necessary. If you keep clean shavings or straw in your nest boxes and clean bedding on the coop floor, you'll have more clean eggs that don't need washing.

Free range chickens

Our office gets your magazine, and everyone so enjoys them. I'm looking for an article on free-range chickens and the difference with the eggs compared to store bought eggs.

Ask Jackie

Could you help me? The article explained how there is good cholesterol in free range eggs and bad cholesterol in store bought eggs. I hope you can help me.

Lillie Savage

Although free range chickens lay eggs that are significantly more nutritious than factory chickens' eggs (which are what you buy in most grocery stores), I wouldn't go as far as to say they were totally free of "bad cholesterol." I believe the vast difference in nutrition, along with much lower fat, in free range chicken eggs is that the happy hens that lay those eggs exercise daily and pick up nutritious wild foods along with feed supplemented by their owner. The caged birds sit, packed five to a small cage, in which they cannot walk or hardly move about, while food constantly is passed in front of them. Mmm. Sounds like the ultimate couch potato, doesn't it?

I have been given hens from a factory such as this. At one year old, the poor hens have slowed down on their "egg a day" and are sent off in trucks to be processed into soup. They huddled in our coop, not knowing how to walk, never having learned to roost. How can these hens lay a healthy egg?

As for facts: factory eggs contain much less carotene, vitamin E, vitamin B-12, vitamin A, folic acid, and omega-3 acids than do free-range eggs, along with having more fat and "bad cholesterol." It makes you glad you have those fat hens scratching out in the yard.

Egg gathering

We thought the May/June issue was exceptional, though we love every issue we get and find something useful every time. We especially enjoyed the article on whole grains, the "Rule of Three," and we always like hearing from Jackie Clay. One thing I would find most helpful when reading articles and letters is to know what part of the country the tips and information comes from. Often weather, climate, or geography makes a difference in whether their way applies to our situation.

... Our chickens are free range, we have solved the problem of them getting in the garden and up on the patio/ decks, but we do not know how to encourage them to lay eggs where we can collect them regularly. We almost never find an egg in their coop though they spend every night in it. They lay everywhere and anywhere and most of the time not in the same place twice, or so it seems; consequently, we do not know how fresh the egg is when we do stumble upon it. Any suggestions?

Rose Umland, California

The best way to get your hens to lay in the nest boxes is to hold them in the coop for several hours in the morning, when most egg laying occurs. I've "trained" the girls to lay in the coop this way. Yes, I still occasionally do find a nest out in the brush. In this case, you can often tell by looking at the eggs about how old they are. If they are relatively clean, they're not so old; if they are all tracked up, they've been there a while. You can check the freshness of the eggs by floating them in a bowl of water. The fresh ones will sink, the not so fresh ones will kind of partly float, and the rotten ones pop to the surface. Always break your questionable eggs in a cup before adding to a recipe. You'll know the bad egg right off; it has a runny white, the yolk is yucky, and if it's really bad, pee-yew!

Speckled, lumpy eggs

I hope you can tell me what is wrong with my chickens' eggs. I have Sex-links and Barred Rocks, The Barred Rocks' eggs are normally cream colored and quite large. Sometimes the eggs look like they are sprinkled with a few grains of red sand, also often times they look like they are spotted with a little blood. The Sex-links' eggs are two toned and they should be plain brown, are very rough feeling with little bumps like very small blisters only they are as hard as the shell, also are spotted with blood. We keep the hens in separate runs so they don't pick at each other, we can't have them free range as the foxes and hawks would have a field day. The eggs look fine inside and taste great but it bothers me that maybe we are doing something wrong.

Ann Krumm, California

I doubt that you are doing anything wrong. Are these young hens? Often pullets that are just starting to lay that have sufficient calcium available, such as oyster shell, can lay bumpy or otherwise "weird" eggs before their bodies get into the swing of egg laying. The blood is probably due to rupturing of tiny blood vessels as the rough egg passes through the oviduct. It is of no consequence. It's like having a little blood on a tissue when you blow your nose. Just make sure they have plenty of water available (sometimes this can be a factor ... but it's usually seen in freezing weather when the chicken pan freezes) and feed as usual. I'm thinking your hens will soon be laying "normal" eggs.

Odd eggs

We've been raising Cornish crosses as meat chickens for several years now, but have been looking for an alternative that would be better at ranging, more healthy, and still produce a nice carcass. We also wanted something that we might be able to winter over so we could breed them naturally and produce our own chicks next spring. I ordered 25 Freedom Rangers, and so far we are really happy with them.

I intended to save two hens and a rooster for breeding. Unfortunately, one of the hens sustained a mortal wound from the rooster's claws during mating. The remaining hen has now started laying eggs, but the shells are extremely soft. I have calcium supplement out free choice, and have switched over to layer feed. Yesterday she appeared to have laid two eggs — one that was just a yolk and one small egg with barely any shell at all (think cellophane).

Is there anything I can do to get "normal" eggshells from her? At first they were soft with extra calcium lumps and bumps on the shell, but they appear to be getting softer rather than harder. She could never sit on a clutch of eggs like that. Or should I cull her now and have a nice roasting chicken?

Carmen Griggs, Minnesota

Sometimes when pullets begin to lay, their laying mechanism is not in sync. Your pullet will probably start to lay more normal eggs as she gets farther into her laying cycle. Keep up the oyster shell and laying mix and she'll probably reward you with nice, hard-shelled eggs.

Ask Jackie

Covering a chicken pen

We have built a chicken house similar to John Silveira's father's in the chickens book (in the garden, left and right chicken doors depending on which side of the garden is fallow). Do I need to provide a covered "pen" for them? They'll be out in the day, in at night, and surrounded by garden fence that is 5 feet high. We have hawks, foxes, and occasionally coyotes. There's supposedly raccoons somewhere, but I've never seen any. We are in a fairly wide open space, and our neighbors dotted around us keep mainly llamas. This is rural Colorado. I believe they'll be safe from most animals, but I would rather not make an outside roof and walls for them using chicken wire mesh, unless I absolutely have to. Sometimes they'll be out after sunset, but always in at night.

Kevin Long, Colorado

Your birds will probably be fine that way, provided that they are shut in at night. Raptors (hawks, primarily) are your worst possible problem. I had one that used to try for my chickens in New Mexico. In fact it would land in the yard and go *inside* the chicken door and chase the chicks around. Until I put our Labrador retriever, Wab, in the coop one day. The hawk landed, hopped boldly into the coop, then flew a lot less cocky out the door and off into the sunset ... with Wab hot on his tail. He never came back, either!

I have no top on my run; in fact, they forage our orchard all day. It's not foolproof, but so far, so good!

Chicken run maintenance

I keep my four laying hens in a fenced in area. It is about a 100-square-foot space. Besides regular raking and general cleaning, is there more I should do to maintain their run, considering the amount of time they spend there?

Greg Scully

Most chickens don't even get so large a run, or any cleaning or raking of their run, so yours are way ahead of most. However, I like to have more than one yard so that they can be alternated. Then you can change the hens to a new yard, till, and plant the old run. This works fertilizer from the chickens into the soil and prevents intestinal parasites from becoming a problem in your birds. It also loosens the chicken-tromped soil. After tilling an old yard, you can either plant it with a chicken crop, such as rye grass or rape (canola) for them to harvest later on, or you can use it as a garden spot for yourself as that chicken manure is great stuff for corn, cabbage family crops, and beans. I wouldn't plant potatoes (overly fertile soil causes scab), tomatoes, or peppers (too much fertilizer will cause them to run to huge plants, but with little fruit).

More details on the kerosene lamp brooder

In the Jan/Feb 2004 BHM, you told how to build a kerosene lamp-heated chicken brooder.

I was not sure of the size of the box. How much room do I need for 25 chicks? We do not have electricity so this is my only way to keep them warm.

Lorraine Warsop, Michigan

We brooded 50 chicks in our kerosene lamp brooder. The box was 18 inches deep, 24 inches long, and a foot high. It had an attached pen on the front that was 18 inches by 4 feet. In this pen was their food and water. On a table nearby, we kept a lantern burning at night to provide light. This prevented them from huddling together and possibly smothering. With the lamp, they pecked and ran around most of the time. The front of the box was hung with a piece of blanket with slits cut in it to hold in the heat, but allowed the chicks to come and go at will.

This brooder worked very well and we only lost one weak chick. Don't forget to have a good layer of sand on the metal bottom to prevent the chicks from getting hot feet from the lamp(s) below.

Chickens in winter

How do your chickens survive (thrive?) in their winter quarters when the weather is below zero? How did our ancestors raise chickens in the cold Wisconsin winters without generators for electricity?

Joyce Andrew, Wisconsin

My chickens are doing great. My coop is pretty much draft-free; I went around with insulation and caulking and filled in all the cracks early in the season. There are enough birds to provide body heat to help heat the coop. I do not provide any type of additional heat, although I would like insulated walls in the coop by next winter. When the snow came, I shoveled it against the walls to help hold the warmth. I also keep plenty of dry shavings on the floor to keep their feet toasty and the dampness down to a minimum. On warmer sunny days, they go outdoors to keep them happy.

Keeping chickens warm in very cold weather

I would like to know how everyone else keeps about 20 chickens warm in the winter when it is 10 or more degrees below zero? You certainly can't run an electric heater with the cost of electricity. How tough are chickens?

Cindy Hills

Chickens are amazingly tough, provided that they are cared for properly. To keep them reasonably warm in the winter, size the coop to the number of chickens you have. With 20 chickens, you won't want a coop much larger than eight by ten feet. Keep the ceiling low, too, to hold in as much warmth as possible. If you are five feet two inches tall, make the ceiling six feet high at max (allowing for bedding buildup).

Give the "girls" plenty of south-facing windows to gather warmth from the sun. Make the coop as tight as possible, yet vent through the roof for some air movement but no drafts. Make double walls, and between them either use commercial insulation or pour dry sawdust, or even staple layers of cardboard in between — anything to provide at least four inches of insulation. More in the ceiling is a good idea. Even fluffy straw in the ceiling is better than nothing when it comes to holding in warmth. Use a storm door, as you do on your house, and tack plastic over the windows during the winter for extra wind protection.

Make sure they have clean, dry bedding. This can be wood shavings, straw, or even ground corn cobs. Scattering a handful of whole corn in the bedding will make the hens dig and scratch for feed. And this will, in turn, do much to warm them up.

Choose a breed with a rose comb. That is a comb that does not stand up, but is tight to the head. Look in poultry catalogs and you'll see the difference. An upright comb will freeze quite easily. Usually this does nothing but cause the comb to turn black and fall off, but sometimes it so stresses the hen that she gets sick and dies.

Give the hens warm water twice a day when the weather is very cold.

Also provide them with a little more corn than normal to give more heating to the body. Extra calories are necessary when it is quite cold.

If you'd like to provide a little more warmth, many farmers simply run a light bulb in the coop, day and night. You'd be surprised how much warmth a 100-watt light bulb provides in an insulated coop.

My chickens are doing just fine in our goat barn this winter, provided with a small "coop in the corner" in which to roost at night in very cold weather. We've had temperatures lower than -43°F and they continue to thrive. But they do have plenty of hay for bedding, a snug barn, and several goat and sheep "heaters" as well.

Nest boxes

Is there a min. or max. size for nest boxes for chickens? What is a good feed mix for hens? I'm not satisfied with the mix that I purchase now even though it is organic, too much dusty stuff.

Kathy Suhr, Washington

The nest box should be large enough for your largest hens to turn around in easily, yet small enough to discourage other hens from trying to enter the nest box when a hen is already sitting in it. Depending on the breed, a nest box of about 12x12 inches works fine (bantams need a smaller nest box; larger breeds, such as Jersey Giants, a larger box).

I feed all my chickens an 18% chopped scratch feed. They lay well on it and eat it happily. If you have scratch feed available, why not provide feeders for both your organic feed and plain scratch feed and let them choose. I agree that many chicken feeds are finely ground and it looks like a chicken would choke on them. You can also dampen the ground feed with either water or milk to make happy chickens.

De-fleaing the coop

I know you have given this advice in the past, but I can't find it in the archives. How do you de-flea a chicken coop? Isn't there a mixture of wood ash and sevin you can use as a dust bath? What is the ratio?

Amy Arthur, Wisconsin

Old timers used powdered tobacco and wood ash, but tobacco is quite toxic, as is Sevin. What I do is buy a box of rotenone garden powder, then hold each hen upside down by the feet and dust her well, especially around the tail and under the wings. Clean your coop well, then dust it as well before putting down fresh shavings. Repeat the individual chicken treatment in a week and your girls should remain mite free.

Ask Jackie

Controlling fleas

It is barely spring and already the fleas are out of control. I have been using DE and it helped until they invaded the chicken coop. There are now thousands and there seems to be no end to their increase. I've read everything on the internet but still have so many especially after I go to gather eggs. Your best suggestions will be appreciated.

Nita Holstine, Texas

Here's what I'd do; I would completely clean out the chicken coop, removing *all* old litter, nest box filler, manure … everything. Then hose down the coop with bleach water; pressure wash it if you have a pressure washer … or you can borrow or rent one. Let the coop dry well, then dust the nests, as well as the floor, with rotenone powder. Also dust the chickens as they roost that night, holding them upside down by the feet so you get their "armpits" and into their feathers. Repeat the dusting in one week and you'll see a dramatic decrease in your little buggers.

Protecting chickens from weasels

My sisters just bought me a subscription to this wonderful magazine and I love it. I have a problem that I really need help with. Every year I raise a fine, healthy flock of hens and a couple roosters and during the winter have to fight the weasels to keep them alive. This is my 3rd year and I am despairing of keeping my precious flock and feel like not doing this anymore. Is there a way to keep the weasels out?

Tami Olsen, Washington

Yes, you can beat the weasels. I had the same trouble on one of our homesteads. First, make your chicken coop tight! A weasel can squeeze through a small hole the size of a quarter. Or a crack in the door. They can also climb like a squirrel, so remember spaces above the doors and windows, too. Pick up debris around the outside of the coop. They hide, breed, and live in wood piles, piles of trash, hollow logs, and brush piles. Remove their hidey holes and it'll help. Get a good barn cat and feed it well so that it'll stay home. I had one spayed female cat that lived in the chicken coop and the weasels disappeared!

In the winter, watch for their tracks in the snow where they might be prowling around the coop at night. If you see them, set rat traps, baited with a little fresh chicken meat. Be sure to tie the trap to something solid so the weasel (white ermine in the winter) will not drag off your trap. Once you get your coop tightened up, you should be about weasel-proof, though.

Homesteading sometimes is frustrating, but the key to anything is persistence. Just keep plugging on and you will succeed in your garden and your life. Read the column and articles here in *Backwoods Home Magazine* and apply all that you feel will work for you. Thousands of folks across the country are making a better life, a self-reliant life, for themselves and their families. Keep on, and you will be one, too!

Muddy chicken run

We've had chickens for a few years and are very grateful for those nice warm eggs every morning. I really want to keep my chickens healthy for a long time. I'm concerned

Ask Jackie

about their run that is so muddy, especially during our rainy season, which in the Pacific Northwest is about half the year.

The chickens have an inner run that leads right into the nice house we built for them. And they also have access to the compost area which is about the same size as their run. After gardening season is over, we let them roam through the garden as well.

On to my questions. Do we just scoop up all that good chicken manure from their inner run and transfer it to the compost heap? How long does it need to "cure" before it's okay to add it to the garden and till it all in? Is it unhealthy to throw their scratch out to them in that squishy muddy area?

They seem fine and healthy and are laying nice eggs, but I just want to keep them healthy for as long as possible.

Ilene Duffy, Oregon

I, too, love the nice warm eggs. In fact, not much feels nicer than holding one of those big warm eggs up to your cheek on a cool morning. Delicious! Something that city people will never know.

Yes, you can add the chicken cleanings to your compost pile. I usually fork the top off a pile, add the chicken manure, then put the cap back on. This hastens decomposition by ensuring quick heating of the pile. Lucky you — with your wet climate, you don't even have to water your pile to make it work!

I have several compost piles in different stages of change, from raw stuff to that black gold we all lust for. I usually figure on the spring pile having had enough time to work to use on the garden as fertilizer in the late fall, if all has gone well. While not black and crumbly at this stage, the manure has decomposed enough so that it isn't so hot it bothers the garden.

Of course, if you've got more time than I do (ha ha ha), you can hurry that compost pile along by turning it regularly, adding more green material (i.e. grass clippings, spent veggies, etc.), and turning it again. Unfortunately, most of us are lucky enough to just get the stuff on the compost pile. Right now I have goat manure composting in the goat pens. Oh well, it has straw on top and helps keep them warm until we get it out in the spring. Not the ideal situation, but we had a busy fall.

Could you get some sand and build up that outside run? It might make it drain better and reduce the squish. However, chickens don't seem harmed by running in the mud. Possibly you could feed them scratch out of a pan, so they didn't have to pick it all up from the mud? It may reduce the possibility of them picking up intestinal parasites.

Goats

Angora goats and rabbits

My husband and I have started raising hair goats and rabbits. I have some concerns as to winter hardiness of these animals, as we live in Montana. I have read that Angora goats need extra protection in the winter, as they are desert animals. What about Angora rabbits? Do Angora goats really need more protection than do my dairy goats? Do Angora rabbits need more protection than normal furred rabbits?

Jacquie Andrews, Montana

I have not found that Angora rabbits or goats need any more winter protection than do other breeds. I had both while living in Minnesota years back. They were kept in the same conditions as were my other dairy goats and rabbits with good results. With any goat, just be sure they have a well-bedded shelter, providing protection from driving rain or snow. In extreme weather, allow several animals to run in the same shelter so they can bunch together for warmth.

Angora rabbits require no different winter housing as do other breeds of rabbits. Just shelter them from wind, drafts, and extreme cold.

Goats for milking

Very soon I'll be going back to the land. I plan on having three goats to start with, one male and two females. My questions may not be in your field.

1. What is the best breed for long term milking?

2. What month do they start coming into heat?

3. I know they carry the young for five months. I would like to have one bred in August so by January I'll have milk all winter, and have #2 goat bred in January. Is this at all possible? My goal is to have milk all year with two goats.

Happy homesteading in Minnesota, and thank you for everything you do for BHM.

Edwin Blood, New Jersey

I think your questions are in my field, as I've raised goats for about 40 years now. In fact, we've got a whole pen full right now.

I don't think there is any one breed that is best for long-term milking. It seems to be more of a hereditary factor. Some families of goats have long lactations, where others only milk well for a couple of months and then slack off. Talk to the breeder of your new girls. Most folks will be quite honest in this regard. Do buy a good dairy goat, not just a cheap goat. There is a huge difference. A good dairy goat should produce at least three quarts of great milk a day for 10 months or longer. A scrub goat may only give enough to feed her kids, then go dry. They eat the same.

Goats can come into heat nearly all year-round, usually skipping the hottest months. Yes, you can breed one in late August and the other in January or February. I do this. My first doe freshened in January this year and the next two will freshen in late May. This is reasonable and only good sense.

You probably don't need a buck at this point. It is much easier to take your does to a good buck, paying a stud fee. In this way, you do not feed or care for him and you can switch bucks, if you would like, to introduce different bloodlines into your little herd. At some point, you may want to buy or trade for a very nice buck, but most new goat owners are better off to use someone else's buck.

Best dairy goats

Seems I read somewhere a goat crossbreed Pygmy/Nigerian made good pets and milk producers. Before I buy my goats, what do you think?

William and Jane Petty, North Carolina

I really prefer larger breeds of dairy goats. They produce more milk for the feed consumed and the excess bucks also can be used for meat, as wethers, either by you or from sales. There isn't much market for pet pygmy goats. But this is a personal decision; some people swear by this cross, as well as purebred Nigerians or Pygmies.

"Goats Produce Too"

I would like to find out where I can purchase a book referenced in the latest issue of BHM. *The book is called "Goats Produce Too" by Mary Jane Toth.*

Sue

I got my copy of *Goats Produce Too* through Hoegger Supply Company, at www.hoeggerfarmyard.com or 1(800)221-4628. It's a great little book and I use it often, especially during the spring and summer cheese making time. Mmm. You've got me thinking about my favorite feta cheese with sun-dried tomatoes and basil.

Storing goat milk

I was planning on getting some goats to milk, so I got your book on dairy goats. Are Nubians the best milkers? I don't have any way to keep things cold (no refrigerator). How long will milk stay fresh without being cold? I plan to build a root cellar, but I don't know if it will keep in there.

Lola Taylor, Georgia

Dairy goats are wonderful. They have great milk and are fun to be around. No, Nubians aren't the "best" milkers. Any good goat of any breed you choose will be a great milker; it doesn't vary with breed. I just like the look of Nubians and the colors. Their milk will keep as long as any milk will. Do you have a spring or creek? Many people keep their foods that need refrigeration in one. Or dig an old freezer down into the ground on the north side of the house in the shade. By stacking a few bales of straw over that, it will help keep food cool much longer than if you just kept it out. I make a lot of yogurt and soft cheeses.

You might try that too for a way of using up the milk and having "free" tasty and varied foods.

Yes, milk will keep longer in a root cellar; not as long as in a refrigerator, but longer than on the kitchen shelf. The old timers often let their cream rise in the cellar to make butter, since it was a cool place.

Salty goat milk

My husband, three children, and I have been on our homesteading journey for only about three years now. My problem is we have several milking goats and they have been doing well. We keep them away from the billy, but every once in a while their milk tastes really bad — like salty and acidic. I can't figure it out. We feed them goat ration with alfalfa pellets, fresh hay everyday, and fresh alfalfa, grass, and sometimes elm leaves. I am not sure what the culprit is.

Jenni Williams, Texas

My guess on your bad tasting milk is that one of your goats may have sub-clinical mastitis; maybe she banged her udder or some other goat butted it. Pick up a California Mastitis Test kit from a local farm store or your vet. If you have bad tasting milk, isolate the goat it came from, even if you have to chill each goat's milk individually. Then test the goat to see. If she does have mastitis brewing, check the milk again the next day. If she still has bad tasting milk, check with the CMT. You may need to give antibiotic injections in the muscle for a few days to clear it up. Early mastitis often doesn't show the "typical" signs, such as bloody or chunky milk, but can taste "off."

Pasteurizing goat milk

I was wondering about pasteurizing goat milk. I buy it from a farm, unpasteurized, in a gallon container from the refrigerator. Once I get it home and do the pasteurizing to 140 degrees, then cooling it to 40 degrees, I just put it back in the jug and stick it back in the fridge? I just want to make sure it's okay to do that since it is already chilled when I buy it. Any info would be greatly appreciated. It is for my six-month-old baby.

Ashley Weh

While milk pasteurizes faster when put into the pasteurizer warm, it's perfectly okay to use the pre-chilled goat milk. The temperature reached for pasteurizing and the length of time used is the same, but you'll notice a longer time-frame for the process.

To be absolutely "safe," are you also sterilizing the original milk jug? (Medically speaking, there could be bacteria "lurking" in the unsterilized jug from the raw milk.) Let me say though, from years of experience with eight children who drank goat's milk, and experience using raw milk, that this is going to the extreme. Provided that the goat (or cow, for that matter) is healthy, having been tested negative for Brucellosis, having no abscesses, and that the milk is handled well from the time of milking to when a person drinks it, I have seen absolutely no problems from drinking it raw.

(Goat abscesses can be from a contagious disease, which can be transmitted through the milk, although I don't believe anyone has shown that it can be passed to humans — only kid goats, drinking the milk.) And before anyone pins my ears back for not mentioning TB, tuberculosis in goats is so extremely rare that it is nearly nonexistent.

I know my own babies who drank both breast milk and raw goat milk picked up a lot more bacteria off toys and their own fingers than they ever did from the milk. Goat milk is great.

Using goats to get rid of brush

We have a small pasture and on one end there is sumac and honey locust we would like to get rid of. The only ideas folks (including the extension agent) have is spraying. Both things spread by runners so brush hogging makes it worse ... Everybody says get goats for brush. What do you recommend in the way of goats? Also fencing for them and guard animals for them? How many would you recommend?

Julia Rader, Arkansas

Yes, you can probably get rid of the sumac and honey locust with the help of goats. I don't know how large your pasture area is, so I can't make a definite recommendation as to how many goats you would need. In most cases, you'll find that even a few goats, say six or seven, will do a lot of good on a relatively small brushy area. You may want to brush hog it down to remove the tough older stems. It won't spread it, but it will come up again. The new shoots will be tender and appealing to the goats.

Have you ever wanted to try dairy goats? If so, this would be an ideal time for you. Any breed will give the same results on your brush. If your only concern is to kill the brush, you can pick up some crossbreeds from a local breeder for a good price.

Here are a few tips for you: an electric fence will not keep goats contained. You can use it to reinforce either stock panel fence or woven wire field fence. This keeps the goats from standing on the fence or eating through it. Both things quickly weaken and sag the wire. I would probably use stock panels attached to T posts and try to hold the goats in the brushy area as much as possible. You may also need to feed them a little hay, depending on how much other feed and grass is available in your mini-pasture. Don't forget a mineral salt block and fresh water every day.

Probably the best guard animals for goats are donkeys and llamas. But they have to be introduced to your herd and become one with it before any guarding will happen. The guards must feel like the goats are part of their family. At any rate, it's a good idea to bring the goats up every evening to be shut up in a small corral with a shed till morning. Most animal predators are more active at night … including stray dogs. Your goats will stay safer that way.

Sheep vs. goats

I've had goats for 35 years. The old retired girls now stay close to home when out on pasture. They are very good watchdogs.

Why are goats a preference to sheep? They have sheep that now produce a fair amount of milk, which will also produce butter — an asset over owning goats. Also sheep are less aggressive and easier to handle and care for.

Received literature on the Dorper sheep, which seem to be a desirable breed. Do you have a preference of breed for milking?

Evelyn, California

Well, first of all, goat teats are much larger, longer, and easier to grip than are sheep teats. Then the wool on the belly of sheep drops debris in the milk bucket at milking time, making them harder to keep clean for milking. I don't find goats aggressive at all. Are your girls horned, by chance? Those horns sometimes make all the attitude difference in the world. I disbud all my kids and have never had a goat that was aggressive toward people.

I use a lot of milk, making yogurt, cheeses, and other dairy products, and haven't been too excited about the production of sheep. I prefer a one-gallon milking doe goat compared to messing with four separate quart producing ewes.

For many people, milking sheep is a fad. For others it is unique and interesting, and that's great. If you want to try milking sheep, go for it. Sheep are nice. We have three Shetland sheep and find them fun and gentle. If you decide to try milking sheep, talk to breeders and visit their flocks at milking time to see what to expect. Then buy a ewe or ewe lamb from higher producing ewes from their farms. You will not be happy with just "any old sheep."

Grain for goats

Is it really necessary to feed grain to your goats? I read in an article that feeding grain was a waste of money and could cause health problems. I'm on a low budget (read that VERY broke!) and don't want to spend a nickel that I don't have to.

Jan Evans, Michigan

Well, your goats won't starve if you don't grain them, provided that they get plenty of access to a good quality pasture or hay. But if you want them to give birth to nice healthy kids, put plenty of milk in the bucket when you milk them, milk for a long lactation, have fewer birthing problems, and fewer breeding problems, I would sure give them a good ration of grain twice a day. No, you don't want your milking does and your buck fat. But by providing a good, balanced diet, you will actually be saving tons of money in the long run. Your does will breed easily, carry and give birth to strong, healthy kids, give you lots of milk, and remain healthier than if you skip the grain. The health problems the article probably referred to is the result of overfeeding grain, which is also not a good idea. Not only can goats develop an acid rumen, but can bloat or even founder. However, these problems are seldom seen as very few people overfeed grain to their goats.

Grain is especially important during the winter when the goats use plenty of calories to keep warm. If you can't afford to grain several goats, consider cutting back your herd to the number of animals you can afford to give grain to. This is often a very wise decision and one which I use myself.

Keeping goats

We will be adding dairy goats to our homestead this spring. I was wondering how much square feet per goat in a shelter?

James Kash, Kentucky

Instead of just quoting a "square feet per goat," let me tell you what works for us. In a 6x12-foot pen, we comfortably house four adult goats or three adults and a couple of partly grown kids. Of course, they have access to large outdoor yards as well. In the past, we had three adult goats in an 8x10-foot mini-barn and that worked out fine. You may be able to "get by" with less room, but we sure like our animals cozy and comfortable. Crowding leads to dirty conditions and health problems.

Goats and poisonous plants

Here I am again! Now I am canning. Thanks to you and your answers to my questions on that. I have another one, on the matter of goats.

I have 12 milk goats at the moment and going to expand as soon as we get moved to our new place in Missouri. It has fruit trees (already bearing). From reading your vet book I know peaches, plums, cherries, and any fruit with a pit is poisonous to them, but what kind of plants and flowers are poisonous?

We will be moving, hopefully, in September or October.
Ron and Bernice Knapp, Kansas

I really wouldn't worry too much about your goats eating poisonous plants. Of course I wouldn't recommend a diet including them, but from my experience most animals can nibble on them without side effects and only get into trouble when there is little but poisonous plants to eat. You see this a lot when the animals are confined to a small pasture. They quickly eat up the good forage, then resort to eating the poisonous plants and become sick or die.

A few plants that you may watch out for include lupine, bracken fern, poison hemlock (along wet areas), choke-cherries, and dock (which is edible in small doses, but can cause problems when consumed in a large amount). Talk to your county extension agent when you get moved to Missouri. He can tell you what toxic plants you may encounter in your county there.

As for the pit fruits, most are toxic in the wilted state if green branches break off in a storm and land in the pasture. Animals can often nibble on the green branches and leaves with no ill effects; mine nibble on chokecherry leaves often. Notice, again, that I emphasize "nibble," as animals cannot make a steady diet of chokecherry without ill effects. Good luck on your new homestead.

Housing and feeding goats

My questions are for the most economical ways to:

1. Feed dairy goats economically. Lots of pasture — but no goats browse remotely close to the house to keep them safe.

2. Provide safe and usable housing for goats for protection and milking location. Any health issues with goats and chickens being close neighbors? Again, predators will likely be a huge deal with neighbor dogs, coyotes and recently spotted wolves (absent in the area since the depression).

Susan Ginnings, Texas

Your goats will do well on pasture. They do not need to browse; they just prefer it. When I had my goat dairy, my goats had a fenced pasture of clovers and orchard grass and did very well. You can also grow a lot of your own feed by growing extra corn, squash, carrots, etc. I also feed my goats leftover green corn stalks, the corn husks, cobs (from canning), and such things as spent pea vines, bean plants, carrot tops, etc. You can also cut your own hay to help feed your herd. Start small and gain experience. It's also cheaper!

Like the chicken yard, use stout goat fence, with the stand-off strands of electric wire to keep the dogs away. Dogs are a worse predator than wolves ever were!

Goats and chickens can live near each other without problems; mine do. Just be sure your chickens can't poop in the goats' drinking water or on their feed.

Pick up a copy of the *BHM* handbook, *Dairy Goats: A beginner's guide*, for more ideas, and the very best of luck in your move!

Cattle

Calves or heifers

Jackie, I'm new into cows. Don't know anything about them. I have 40 acres of pasture land. What should I start with, a handful of calves or heifers with calves on the ground or bred heifers?

Kevin Brown, Mississippi

I think if I were you, I'd start with some calves for the reason that they are easier to handle, especially when you aren't used to cattle. Adult cattle can be wild-acting and challenge fences. Speaking of fences, I'd also advise getting your pasture fenced with at least four strands of barbed wire or woven field fence, plus a top strand of either electric or barbed wire, before getting your calves. That way, you'll be ready for them when they get past the "baby calf" stage and need that pasture. And calves grow very fast. Our late summer baby calves are now nearly 500 pounds and their backs are up to my shoulder.

Training a milk cow

I have a new milk cow. We purchased her a month ago and she gave us her first calf last night. She has never been hand milked. I've been reading a lot on how to train a milk cow, and I understand training by repetition and routine, but some questions seem to stay at the top of the unanswered list ... What specifically can I do to make this cow feel easy/safe around me? How do I keep her flight zone small? How do I teach her to accept me and allow me to milk her with ease? I don't want it to be a bad experience for her. I see others whose cows don't even flinch, their backs don't "jump" when petted. I want to get to that point, and don't know how.

Marilyn Lakaner, Missouri

The best way to settle her down and "break" her to milk is to get her into a stanchion or tie her firmly in a corner. Then, while feeding her some grain, begin brushing and petting her. Work first on her neck and shoulders if she seems "kicky." You'll tell she's settling down when she stops swishing her tail and moving around. Do this twice a day and work on both sides of her. As she quiets down, brush and pet down her sides to her udder. Work firmly, but gently, as some cows are ticklish on their bags and teats. It's natural for her to push you away from her bag with her back feet or even swing a kick at you. That's how cows keep other cows' calves from sucking on them. If she just pushes at you with her hind legs, block her push with your arm and continue talking to her and touching her.

Are you milking her, now that the calf is born, or are you letting it suck? It's probably a good idea to pen the calf and teach the cow to accept you as the "milker" instead of the calf. You can bottle feed the calf after you milk, or let the calf nurse when you're about two quarts from being finished as a "reward" for being good. Every cow is different in this respect. Some hold their milk for the calf and that gets old. If that's the case, just bottle-feed the calf.

If she is very kicky and determined not to let you milk, you may have to either use an anti-kicking device such as a back restraint or hobbles. Working with such a cow can be frustrating, but hold your temper and just keep doing what you must to get the job done. And keep petting and brushing her. She will almost always come around and become the gentle sweet cow you wanted.

Playful cow

We have raised organic beef and dairy cattle for years. Now we are raising a Brown Swiss dairy calf for a future family milk cow. She's 5 months and very playful to the point of being dangerous. (butting, etc.) We handle her daily. Should we get her a companion as cows are a herd animal? We have never raised one by herself before.

Arlene, New York

I would advise carrying a small stick about a foot long and an inch in diameter into the pen every time you go in. When your heifer comes to you and gets "happy," trying to butt at you, rap her across the bridge of her nose with this stick. At the same time, tell her "back!" Then step toward her and tell her "back!" again. If she doesn't immediately step back, rap her nose again. This type of training only takes a couple of times before she begins to respect you and understand that she shouldn't run up and butt or shove you. Another animal about her size would be enjoyed by her and maybe give her a place to wear off some of her playfulness. But she should still respect you and obey the command "back."

Castrating bull calves

We raise a few livestock, mainly for home use. We have a bull calf that we are keeping for beef. We were told to wait to castrate him when he was about 500 pounds, which he is now. I don't know whether that was a wise decision. I need your advice. What is the best method to castrate and since we don't have a chute, how is the best way to restrain the animal? I was told you had written a book on home vet work. If so, please let me know how to get it and how to castrate our bull.

Larry Estep, Virginia

Whew! I'd get the guy who advised you to wait till your calf weighed 500 pounds to come over, and hold him while you castrate him. (I mean the bull, now!) I usually castrate our bull calves, meant for beef, at about 150 pounds, where I can handle them nearly single-handed without a chute or cowboy.

I revised *A Veterinary Guide for Animal Owners*, which my late husband and I wrote 20 years ago. You can get this book from *BHM*. In it are described several methods of castration. The one I much prefer is the use of a "clamp" which pinches the blood vessels and effectively castrates the calf with no blood or cutting involved. It is not the "band" method, where a strong rubber band is slipped up over the scrotum, cutting off all circulation. This can be dangerous, as tetanus and infections following this method of castration are all too common.

What I would recommend is that you have a veterinarian who has a portable chute come out and do the deed. These chutes tow behind a truck like a trailer. The bull calf is corralled, roped, or herded into the chute where he can be safely handled and castrated.

If this is impossible, I'm afraid I'd make young beef out of your bull before he gets too big for his britches, escaping from home and causing neighbor trouble, as they will often do. Next time, "pinch" that bull calf when he is much smaller and easier handled.

I have castrated such large bulls by roping them, haltering the animal with a stout halter, tying him to a fence post of a plank or pipe corral, then closing a strong gate up on his free side. With several helpers, one to hold the gate tight against the bull's side by using a rope behind his butt tied to the center of the gate, then run to a fence post on the other side for leverage, and another strong, fearless helper to hold the base of the bull's tail straight up over his back with as much power as he can muster, we can immobilize his hind legs to a great extent. Then he may be castrated with the Burdizzo clamps. Never clamp both testicles at once. You must never clamp across the center division between the testicles. Do one at a time instead.

Again, this is not a safe procedure, and carries risk of injury. But I have done it several times when there was no other alternative available. I'd call the vet, myself. Good luck.

Some cautions about castrating older bulls

At what age or weight would you not castrate a bull? I usually band newborns when they are a few days old. I have some that I have bought and wonder what chances I have of losing them if I castrate. Their weight is from 150 to 1,200 pounds.

K. Bishop

It is certainly possible to castrate any size bull. But I would not band a larger animal. There is much danger of tetanus with a bigger animal, as the wound is larger (yes, there is a wound where the band cuts into the flesh, causing the testicles to become necrotic and drop off) than in a newborn calf.

I prefer to use a Burdizzo emasculator on larger animals. This pinches the cord and blood vessels, which causes the testicles to shrink and the animal to become sterile. There is no wound, no bleeding, and no shock. If you don't have, or can't borrow this "clamp," you might consider having your vet come out for those big bulls. Or butcher them as bulls. The meat is not affected by being left entire.

If you do use the clamps, never attempt to do both testicles at the same time. You must isolate and clamp one cord, leading to one testicle, at a time. This requires two pinches with the emasculator.

Best method of castration

I am a small farmer and raise a few calves to keep the pasture cleaned up. I saw where you revised the "Veterinary Guide for Animal Owners." I keep steers and sometimes I buy bull calves and have to have them castrated.

I would like some information on castrating calves; the best method and so on. I would like to be able to do this myself.

Larry C. Estel, Virginia

There is no reason you cannot learn to castrate bull calves yourself. After spending more than 20 years as a veterinary field technician, I much prefer using a Burdizzo. This is a totally bloodless, relatively painless method of castration. There is no chance of infection and it's quite easy, when done right.

The Burdizzo is basically a large pinching clamp with long handles to increase leverage for the operator. With the calf adequately restrained, the testicles are taken in one hand, while the Burdizzo is held in the other. The operator makes sure the clamp only is placed over the cord leading to one testicle. Never clamp across the septum, the division between the testicles. Likewise, never include a portion of the testicle in the clamp's jaws. Carefully position the Burdizzo above one testicle, cord in the center, well away from the center division, then close the handles, completing the clamp. Hold the Burdizzo in this position while you count to ten, then release. Repeat the process with the other testicle.

When you are finished, the only sign of the castration will be a slight indentation where you clamped. It is wise to check, as the few "slips" (failed castrations) I've seen with the Burdizzo were often because the operator clamped the same testicle twice.

You might pick up a copy of *A Veterinary Guide for Animal Owners* (sold by *BHM*) for illustrations and information on this subject.

Ask Jackie

Is my steer really a steer?

My son will be taking a steer to our county fair. He was banded soon after we bought him in September 2003. He weighed about 450 to 500 lbs. My daughter's steer was banded as a calf. They do not look the same when you look from behind and we are afraid that my son's steer may not actually be a steer. How can we know for sure if he is steered without calling the vet? We have felt both and they feel about the same. Would there be a big difference in the way they look and feel if one was only partially castrated?

Renee Dyer

The most sure way to tell if your "steer" is a steer is to have someone restrain him and feel the scrotum. With a bull, you can easily feel each testicle roll about inside. There is no doubt at his age. If he has testicles, he is an entire male. His body appearance will also be more masculine. His head will look wider and stronger, as will his neck and shoulders. He will also be beginning to act like a bull, digging dirt with his head, rumbling deep in his throat when he "talks," and sniffing the behinds of other cattle.

I much prefer using an emasculatome or Burdizzo on male animals, especially older males, as banding older males can sometimes fail due to the bulk of the part being contained by the band. The emasculatome, or "pincher," crushes the blood vessels and cords, one at a time, producing a bloodless, quick, and nearly painless castration. There is also very, very little chance of infection, unlike banding. Banding causes the part to drop off, leaving a raw wound which can become infected. I've seen many banded animals with tetanus from using rubber bands as a castration method, and none with the Burdizzo.

If you still can't decide about your "steer," I'd suggest having the 4-H leader or a neighboring cattleman come have a look. If they can't give you a thumbs up, it's time to call your vet.

Bitter milk

I have just started milking and the flavor of the milk is bitter. I pasteurize but the odor, smell, and taste were there before I pasteurized. It must be what she is eating because I can smell the same odor on her breath when she chews her cud. Any ideas? I am very disappointed since I planned to make cheese, butter, ice cream, etc.

Deb Hemingway

Well, Deb, let's find out why your milk is awful so you can fix the problem and get to those dairy goodies. My first impression is like yours; it very well could be something she is eating. To test this theory, pen her up in a dry lot for a week, only feeding hay and a corn/oats mixture. Some dairy animals cannot be fed molasses, as their milk gets an off flavor.

After a week, check the flavor of the milk. If it is now good, you know it definitely was something she was eating that affected the taste of the milk. If her dairy grain has molasses, add that back to her diet. Then check the milk. If it is still good, you know it wasn't that.

Walk her pasture and look for plants that could cause off flavored milk: wild mustard, anything in the cabbage family (kale, rape, etc.), wild garlic, wild onions, etc. Break plants off and smell them. If you notice "that" odor, you know you have the culprit. You will now have to rid your pasture of that plant or keep her fenced off from patches of the culprit.

Another cause of off-flavored milk is low grade, chronic mastitis. This often shows up at freshening and is characterized, in many cases, as only a few "creamy chunks" caught in the milk filter. Mastitis can be treated by milking the udder completely out several times a day and treating her with intramuscular antibiotics.

If the diet did not cause the problem, talk to your veterinarian. There are several problems, including mastitis, that can cause bad flavored milk. She may need a check up.

Is your dairy animal a goat? If so, some does produce "goaty" flavored milk. This can usually be corrected by giving free choice baking soda in a pan in the feed trough. After several days you will often notice good, sweet milk just like you dreamed of.

Your trouble is not rare, but it isn't common either. I'll bet with some sleuth work you can find the problem. Good luck.

Raw cow's milk

I have been thinking about purchasing a cow for milk but would like to know if it is safe to drink milk right from the cow or should it be processed somehow?

Julie Guenter, Texas

If drinking raw milk would harm me, I'd be dead. I've consumed raw cow and goat milk for more than 40 years and much prefer it to "processed" store milk. Yes, you can pasteurize it, but that kills some of the beneficial enzymes in it.

Make sure your cow is well cared for and has been tested for brucellosis and T.B.

I feel that there are certainly a lot more things to worry about in our daily diets today, with all the chemicals, herbicides, fertilizers, insecticides, preservatives, genetically engineered foods, etc., than drinking raw, fresh milk from a healthy, well cared for family cow.

Hamburger tastes bad

We butchered a beef and took it to the butcher where he let it hang 23 days. Now the hamburger tastes bad. Could it be that it was hung too long and the fat got a foul taste?
Diane Grover

I just had a good discussion about your problem with our butcher, Steve, at the Cascade Meat Market.

Steve's been in the packing business for years and is like a surgeon with his meat. None better. We never let our meat hang longer than 14 days, but Steve says that under good, regulated, cold locker conditions, 21 days is okay. But any less than ideal conditions and 23 days would be just too long.

If there is any outside rancid fat that is not removed, leaving even a small piece of it to be ground in with the lean meat when making hamburger can ruin the taste of the whole batch. While the hamburger would still be "edible" if cooked well, you will probably have to season it very well to eat it. This is why Third World countries eat so much highly seasoned meat; it covers the slightly "bad" taste in nearly spoiled meat, which occurs because of lack of refrigeration.

Another source of nasty tasting hamburger is freezer burn. You didn't say how old your hamburger was. If it is more than a year old, regardless of how well wrapped, it will develop freezer burn and be pretty disgusting to eat. This is one reason I can most of our meat.

How much beef?

How can I find out approximately how many pounds of packaged beef I would have after having a 1,000-lb. steer killed and processed?

Janet Lucas

Well, Janet, that's kind of like asking, "How long is a string?" There are many variables: breed, age, type of feed provided, type of cuts (i.e. boneless vs bone-in), who does the processing, etc. For instance, if you butcher a 1,000-pound Jersey steer, you will receive back much less meat than if you butcher a 1,000-pound prime Angus steer. Dairy breeds yield more bone in the bone-to-meat ratio than do beef breeds. This certainly is not to say that dairy breed beef is worthless. It is very good. You will just get fewer pounds of actual meat per carcass.

But, as a rough estimate, a prime Angus steer will lose about 30% of live weight in bone, head, legs, etc. As most butchers hang the carcass for a week or more to aid tenderness, you can figure on losing another 3%-4% as the meat also dehydrates slightly.

So, realistically speaking, your prime Angus 1,000-pound steer might yield about 650 pounds of packaged meat. A nice, but not prime, beef steer would probably yield 575 pounds. Remember, there is a lot of give and take here. Find a butcher you can trust and let him process your steer.

Home-raised beef is really great, not like most tough, taste-less supermarket cuts.

Caring for a dairy cow

I want to have a couple of dairy cows so that I will have enough milk for my family. How much milk will this one particular breed give me on a daily basis? What do I feed her/them? What kind of shelter do I need? What equip-ment do I need for milking? What about daily and annual care requirements? Where do I get all this stuff? I have been doing a lot of research on the Internet, at the local library, new and used bookstores, have contacted various associations ... and the only conclusion that I have come up with is that I am going to have to work damn hard, and will make a lot of mistakes simply because it is virtually impossible to find the needles.

Lisa Evers, North Carolina

Lisa, having your own dairy cow is nowhere near as com-plicated as you may think. If it was, we sure wouldn't have a milk-cow-in-training right now (a two year old heifer). We have always had a milk cow or two, and we had many dairy goats at one time, which were as good as a cow for all dairy purposes.

My day with a cow goes like this: Morning, give hay to cow and clean up manure. In the winter she is kept in a stanchion with a wood platform raised to allow an 18-inch deep by 18-inch wide gutter behind her to keep the urine and manure off her body when she lays down. Plenty of straw bedding keeps her comfortable. She goes out for ex-ercise during the day, and returns in the late afternoon on all but the coldest, blizzard days. I carry out two buckets, one with warm water and a clean cloth to wash her udder, and a larger stainless steel milk bucket.

After she is watered and her bedding cleaned, she is munching hay happily. I wash her teats with warm water and let them air dry while I get her grain and dump it into her manger.

Then I sit down on her right side, facing her, lean my head into her warm belly, and begin milking. The first stream from each teat is sprayed into the washing cloth to make sure there are no clots or blood streaks, which could indicate mastitis, a common dairy animal infection.

When all teats check out okay, I milk her, two teats at a time, in rhythm. It doesn't matter what breed of cow you choose; even a tame beef breed provides more than enough for family use. Pick one that you like and is used to being hand-milked. When I have enough milk for my needs, I turn her calf with her to finish. Most of my cows will raise not only their own calf but at least three calves I buy at the sale barn each year, in rotation, as they are weaned. The benefit of having a calf available to nurse is that you don't have to be tied down to a milking routine. If you plan on going away for a day, just leave the cow in a pen with the calf or turn them out on summer pasture together.

The fresh warm milk is then strained, either through a commercial milk strainer (available at most feed stores or ranch supply stores) or a sterilized old tea towel (don't wash them in scented detergent).

The cow is milked morning and night. She is fed plenty of good grassy pasture, plus alfalfa or clover/grass hay in the winter, a dairy cow mixed ground feed or high protein sweet feed, depending on your preference. She needs access daily to a mineral-salt block. All feed and most equipment can be bought locally and relatively inexpensively.

Having any animal requires work, but a cow is not a big job and most folks find having one very relaxing. Besides, you will have homemade whipped cream, cheeses, butter, sour cream, ice cream, and even beef if you raise a steer calf each year to butcher when it is two or three. All will be much better than any store-bought products, and they won't make you glow in the dark. Plus you'll have manure to add to your garden's compost pile.

Ducks, geese, sheep, llamas, pigs, and butchering

Breeding ducks

I have a wonderful flock of Muscovy ducks that I started raising last year. My question is about breeding. Is it a good idea to introduce "new blood" to prevent inbreeding? Or is it a problem? Should I obtain new birds from outside the flock occasionally?

Jack

Yes, it is a good idea to introduce a new male from outside the flock from time to time. This goes for almost any breed of bird. The easiest ways are to simply trade males with a neighbor or give your drake to someone and buy a younger male from a different bloodline.

Raising feeder geese

We are interested in raising feeder geese. Got any info or tips and do they get along with chickens and turkeys?
G. and H. Williams, Mississippi

They get along just fine, provided that they have a large enough pen/coop. Geese and other waterfowl are water lovers, and therefore love splashing and bathing in any and all water available to them. This includes drinking pans/waterers. It makes a heck of a sloppy mess inside a smaller coop. Chickens are not water lovers and can easily become sick from too much dampness. If you have plenty of room, both inside and out, you'll have no problems raising geese with your chickens and turkeys.

Raising and eating geese

We may raise geese this year. I'd like ideas, recipes, anything on how to have a top-quality roast goose.
Karen Burkholder, Virginia

Under the right circumstances, geese are a terrific addition to the homestead. The baby goslings are quite hardy, growing quickly past the need-extra-heat stage. And once they've grown, they do well on a little grain plus grazing, making them economical homestead mini-livestock.

I say "under the right circumstances" because geese can be a pain in the hindquarters sometimes. They can be aggressive, biting and flapping at you with their wings, especially territorial ganders. And they are known to leave huge piles of goose you-know-what in the front yard or even on the doorstep. This is one reason geese are not encouraged to graze on river banks of local parks.

You can raise geese happily, however. One of the best ways is to fence your small orchard or bramble patch and let the geese roam freely in there, having a small shed to go into at night (to escape predators, such as owls). They will keep walkways and the grounds beneath fruit trees nicely "mowed" and free from bugs. Their fertilizer leavings will only enhance the plant and tree growth. The fence will keep them contained so they will not be a nuisance or even a danger to small children. Give them fresh water and a little grain each day and they'll happily grow and grow.

Now for that perfect roast goose! To begin the roast goose, start a couple of months before you plan on eating it. Ease off the corn, so the goose doesn't build tons of fat. Goose is a bit greasy anyway, and you don't want to compound the problem. Feed it grain, but use a mixed grain, such as oats, barley, and a little corn instead of all corn.

When you dress the goose, remove any fat you can find. Usually this will be gobs of fat on the inside, around body organs. Take it all out.

Never roast the goose with the back resting on the roasting pan bottom; it'll end up greasy. Use a rack, elevated by wads of aluminum foil, or even just a few wads of foil alone. This will let the grease drip off the goose and drain into the pan so it doesn't accumulate in the meat. Baste the meat very lightly, for the same reason.

Once the goose has roasted, let it stand for ten minutes before you slice the meat. It will then slice nicely, instead of falling into a pile of shreds. I usually make my stuffing separate from the goose so it doesn't become heavy. If you roast the stuffing with the neck and giblets to give it flavor, it won't become greasy and heavy. You can remove the neck and giblets before you serve it if you wish.

Raising pigs

Have you raised pigs before? If so what breed would you recommend? We just bought three six-week-old mixed breed piglets. Two are uncastrated males. The owner said he never castrates, just butchers them at four months of age, before they are ready to breed. Do you recommend I castrate them? Research on the internet has led me to believe the meat will have a bad flavor if they are around a female. I could sell the female and leave them intact. What are your thoughts?

Mia Sodaro, California

I've raised a lot of pigs, and yes, the meat of older boar pigs does have a flavor I sure don't like. If you castrate your males, they won't have any off taste. If you butcher them at or before four months of age, they'll taste fine, but that seems like a waste because in just a few more months, you'll harvest a lot more meat. Selling the female won't make the boar meat taste any better. Castrating baby pigs isn't difficult or dangerous for them if you follow directions carefully (check out my book *A Veterinary Guide For Animal Owners* available through *BHM*). Or have an experienced person or your vet do it the first time so you can learn by observation.

The breed of pig you raise for meat isn't critical; I've had several and could not decide on a "best" breed. Yorkshires, Duroc, and Hampshires are all commonly-raised, lean-type hogs that make great homestead meat.

How long to hang meat?

Hi, I was just wondering the reason for hanging meat for a period of time and for how long? For example, moose meat.

Rob Gibeault

The reason for hanging meat is that the enzymes in the meat begin to break down tougher fibers in the meat, making it more tender. In effect, this is the pre-spoilage stage; if the meat hangs too long, it will begin to decay. This is why you hear so many reports of "gamey" tasting meat. It has simply hung too long, often with little or no care. You can't hang an animal in a tree out in the sun, especially when the temperature fluctuates to the 40s or even 50s during the day, then dips lower at night, for days on end. This is even worse when the animal was not properly cleaned out and skinned. (You sure wouldn't go buy a nice roast from the store and do that, huh?)

Another reason we hang our meat is so that I can cut it into workable chunks to jerk and can. For instance, I've found that I can quarter a deer or moose and process one forequarter, plus the backstrap in one day, a hind quarter in another day, the neck and tenderloins another day, and so on.

In optimum conditions, say in a locker plant, meat can be hung for 14 days. We don't have these conditions at home, so we try to get our meat to hang about seven days before processing. But that is with the weather cooperating, of course. If it turns unexpectedly warm, we process that meat right now, rather than risk having off-flavored meat or spoilage.

For this reason, we also hunt only when the weather is favorable. I've passed up many a game animal because the day was getting too warm for good meat handling, no matter how fast I field dressed it and got ice into the body cavity.

In really cold weather, your meat can hang longer, but it is hard to cut up frozen carcasses unless you use a chain saw, axe, or good hand saw.

Bleeding out an animal

Can you "bleed out" an animal by slitting its throat just as effectively after it has been shot, or does it have to be alive when you do it?

My husband and I are in disagreement on this issue. I think it is cruel to kill an animal by slitting its throat and letting it bleed to death. He believes that in order for the heart to pump out all the blood, it has to be done this way? Does it?

Lisa Light-Abrego, Michigan

You're both right in my opinion. I couldn't cut a live animal's throat, although many people do just that, in order to get more thorough bleeding out. Generally, most people first shoot the animal, then quickly cut the throat. If this is done quickly, the animal will bleed out enough before it is dead, dead.

What about when you hunt and shoot a deer? You usually don't slit the throat on a live deer. Right? And the meat is just fine.

Butchering 12 pigs in high heat a bad idea

We slaughtered 12 pigs yesterday morning and hung them overnight. This morning we will be doing the cutting and wrapping. Yesterday's temp reached almost 79 degrees but pretty windy. We hung the split sides in our pole barn to firm up overnight. The temps overnight stayed in the mid 60s. Is their any concern that the meat may be compromised due to the temps? We are located in rural Kansas.

Chris Needham

Why you butchered 12 hogs when it was going to be so warm is the question that comes to my mind first off. I much prefer to wait until a very cool day, even freezing. And I never butcher more than one or two animals at once, as I don't have the help to get them taken care of and cut up in a timely manner.

Freshly butchered meat needs to be cooled down pronto. This can be done by rinsing well with cold water or even wiping out with snow if water is unavailable. In warmer weather, filling the body cavity with ice and covering the carcass to hold in the cold helps keep it cool.

Pork, being so fatty, tends to sour quickly when not cooled properly. I sure hate to tell you to throw away 12 pigs' worth of meat, but I really wouldn't want to come to a roast pork dinner when you were serving one of them.

Disposing of large animals

I would like to keep a couple horses and cows, but have never had large animals before. What do you do when they die? Is there an established way to remove the carcass? Do you just pick a quiet corner of your property and bring in a bulldozer? I have heard vaguely that some people will call canning factories for dog food or some such.

Rose K., New Mexico

Death is a fact of life for us all. Fortunately, very few animals die on the farm. Usually one sells an older cow, or a person sells an older horse to buy a younger one before they are beyond use. Of course, some of us old softies keep favorite animals until they die. We just recently lost our old Morgan stallion at age 25. While in many places, you can simply call a rendering plant which renders dead live-stock down into fertilizer and soap fat among other things, we feel that our big "pets" deserve better. A friend brought over a backhoe, and in 10 minutes dug a nice deep grave for our old friend and that was that. He even put up the wood cross that our son, David, made for the horse that taught him to ride.

Farmers with large acreages and living in areas free of restrictions usually just drag dead livestock out into the woods and let nature take its course. (Assuming that the animal did not die of a disease that could be contagious.)

Getting lanolin from sheep

I have searched and searched online for an answer to my question. I hope that you can either answer my question or direct me to someone who can. I have just sheared a very large sheep and he had a couple of years' growth of beautiful gray wool. I would like to harvest the lanolin from this wool. How do I do it? I thought of soaking it in hot water and hopefully the lanolin would rise to the top ... I'm not sure what to do and don't want to lose that valuable stuff. I enjoy your column and my prayers have been with your family since the loss of your dear husband.

Tamara Bock, California

To extract lanolin from sheep wool, all you have to do is boil the wool. The oil that rises to the top of the tub is lanolin. Skim it off, then reheat it to make it thin and strain it through a cheese cloth to remove impurities. You can best boil the wool in large galvanized wash tubs or half metal barrels over an outdoor fire. Some lanolin will rise from wool soaked in quite hot water, although not as much as when you boil it. When you boil wool, it sometimes shrinks and is ruined for spinning. But the wool that has been left on sheep for two years is often not clean enough for spinning because it requires a tremendous amount of work washing and carding to remove the dirt, hay chaff, and pasture seeds. So this may be a good year to make your homemade lanolin!

Llamas as dairy animals

I greatly enjoyed Jackie Clay's article on "Hard Core Homesteading." But I am wondering how, and where, llamas can fit into the picture. I have heard that llamas are better to raise than cows because they take less space and are also "browsers" like goats and deer. Can llamas be used for milk, like cows? Perhaps Jackie could do some research on the subject and let us know. I would be interested to see an article on the subject.

Cara Ebner, Arizona

I truly love llamas, and am a former llama owner. They are neat, friendly, intelligent animals with wonderful wool. They make great sheep guardians and low-impact pack animals. But they are really not much of a dairy animal. First of all, their teats are only about an inch and half long, making them a "treat" to milk. I've done it for newborn crias (baby llamas), and wouldn't recommend it. Instead, why don't you consider dairy goats. They take much less space and feed than a llama and are low-impact animals.

As a hardcore homesteader, an animal must "pay for itself" or be classified as a pet. If you can afford a pet, great. I've got some, myself. (We even had a crippled turkey vulture for three years who insisted on the best brand of dog food.) Llamas make great pets, plus you can use the wool if you hand spin and they will carry your burdens on pack trips. But they just don't make the grade, with me, as a dairy animal.

Pekin ducks and gardening

I thought it would be fun to have a few ducks ... Pekin ducks like in BHM *(Issue #124, July/Aug 2010). I thought they may offer us some eggs and eat some bugs as they run around and look cute.*

But then I started to wonder if they would just fly over the fence and fly away. Would they? And, if so, can their wing feathers be trimmed to keep them grounded? And I wondered if they would also eat the sprouts as the seeds pop up in the spring. Any suggestions?

John (and son) Mason Zimmerman, Georgia

Pekin ducks grow to be large and heavy and I've never had one fly, but you certainly can clip the flight feathers on the wings, keeping them earth-bound. That's what we have to do for our turkeys. Yes, they will eat sprouting seeds. So when the seeds and plants are young, you'll have to plan on penning your ducks elsewhere. Once the plants are large, they shouldn't cause too much damage. Remember that ducks do make large piles of you-know-what that is not nice to step or kneel in. You might want to consider that when permanently fencing your ducks in your garden. As temporary residents, they are great, eating plenty of weeds and bugs.

Dog and cat food recipes

With grocery prices going through the roof and us living on a tight budget, I have been worrying about my three dogs. I see on the news every day where people have to give up their pets because they are unable to feed them. So far this had not been a problem for us as of yet. So to plan ahead, I was looking for homemade dog and cat food recipes. So far the ones that I have found would be expensive to make. So I was wondering if you could give me any dog and cat food recipes for people on a budget.

Trena Stutts, Tennessee

There are a lot of ways people have fed their pets during depressions and other tough economic times. I know one elderly woman who shot woodchucks all summer, then canned them up to feed her little fox terrier. Talk about ingenuity! Also, one of my bosses at a riding school had three watchdogs that he turned into the barns at night. Every morning, that thrifty German brought an ice cream pail full of bones from the butcher and scraps from his evening meal, bread crusts, day-old buns from the thrift store, and any vegetable peels or pieces his wife saved. He'd pour all this, plus a few potatoes, an onion, and carrots from the garden into a steel pail, then simmer the whole works all day on the woodstove. The whole "stew" was thickened with a couple handfuls of cornmeal or rolled oats. At lunch time, the dogs' dinner smelled better than my lunch bucket! And the dogs stayed fat, shiny, and healthy.

With today's prices of soybean meal, cornmeal, etc. it is expensive to make a good pet food. We just buy a good, economic commercial food. But if times get really tough, I'll make stew to feed my dogs and cats, just like my old boss did.

You'll want all eight books in this great Ask Jackie series:

- ❋ Animals
- ❋ Canning Basics
- ❋ Food Storage
- ❋ Gardening
- ❋ Homestead Cooking
- ❋ Homesteading
- ❋ Pressure Canning
- ❋ Water Bath Canning

About the author

Jackie is a lifelong homesteader. From the tender age of three, she dreamed of having her own land, complete with chickens and horses. Learning life skills such as canning, gardening, and carpentry from her mother, father, and grandmother, she slowly became a very experienced homesteader. She has more than 45 years of experience foraging wild foods, growing a garden, raising homestead animals such as goats, cattle, horses, pigs, and, of course, chickens. Jackie cans hundreds of jars of gourmet-quality, homegrown food every single year. The family eats like kings!

She lives on a wilderness 120-acre homestead with her husband, Will (also a lifelong homesteader), and son, David. They raise nearly 90% of their own food and strive for a more self-reliant, off-grid lifestyle.

Jackie has written for many years for *Backwoods Home Magazine,* doing both feature articles on all aspects of low-tech homesteading as well as the informative Ask Jackie column since 1999. She also maintains a popular "Ask Jackie" blog at the magazine's website, www.backwoodshome.com/blogs/ JackieClay. She has also written several books including *Growing and Canning Your Own Food, Jackie Clay's Pantry Cookbook,* and *Starting Over,* as well as several more on animal care.